CHUTZPAH

The maverick mindset for success

YANKY FACHLER

author of **Fire in the Belly**

OAK TREE PRESS
19 Rutland Street, Cork, Ireland
www.oaktreepress.com

© 2006 Yanky Fachler

A catalogue record of this book is
available from the British Library.

ISBN 1 904887 08 2

Printed in Ireland by ColourBooks.

This book is dedicated to my family,
fellow-graduates of
the School of Chutzpah:
my parents Eli and Chava,
my siblings Mordechai, Chaim,
Melanie, Meir and Yossi,
my sons Ashi and Amiti,
my grandson Uri, and Mona.
In memory of David Fachler.

Contents

Chapter 1

Introduction

George Bernard Shaw wrote:

> *The reasonable man adapts himself to the world.*
> *The unreasonable one persists in trying to adapt*
> *the world to himself. Therefore all progress*
> *depends on the unreasonable man.*

It's unlikely that GBS knew the word, but I'm convinced that he was talking about chutzpah.

In the middle of the 19th century, the celebrated social philosopher John Stuart Mill wrote:

> *The amount of eccentricity in a society has*
> *generally been proportional to the amount of*
> *genius, mental vigour, and moral courage it*
> *contained. That so few now dare to be eccentric*
> *marks the chief danger of the time.*

I don't think Mill knew the word chutzpah either, but I'm convinced that he was really describing chutzpah (or the lack thereof)

Before we define chutzpah, let's have an enunciation break:

- ◆ The ch in chutzpah is pronounced like the ch in Loch Ness (or in Fachler).
- ◆ The utz in chutzpah rhymes with the word puts (as in "he puts on the kettle")
- ◆ The pah in chutzpah is pronounced like the pah in oom-pah-pah.

The meaning of this wonderfully evocative and rich word, that has no exact translation in English, is elusive. According to criminal appeals lawyer, Professor Alan Dershowitz of Harvard Law School, who had the chutzpah to call his autobiography *Chutzpah*, the word is more easily demonstrated than defined. He describes chutzpah as a special brand of courage that defies conventional wisdom and conventional logic.

Chutzpah, says Dershowitz, is a go-for-it attitude that envisions possibilities that no one else yet believes are viable, a willingness to demand what is due, to defy tradition, to challenge authority, to raise eyebrows.

Addressing graduates of the Technopreneurship & Innovation programme at Singapore's Nanyang Technological University, guest speaker Mr Teo Ming Kian urged them to develop "the spirit of chutzpah - the sense that everything is possible, and all you need is to try."

I have heard it said that it takes chutzpah to walk around with a name like Yanky Fachler. A throwaway comment in my direction *apropos* my name, "Your parents have a lot to answer for," even served as the opening salvo in a courtship that blossomed into a permanent romantic attachment.

I'm a Yanky who wasn't born in the land of the Yanks. Despite having been born, bred and educated in England's Home Counties, my accent has been variously described as sounding Swedish, Australian, South African and German. I once received a letter from the British Council. They obviously assumed I was Scandinavian, because the letter was addressed to Mr Jan Key.

I can testify that, like Ben Stiller's Fokker character in *Meet the Parents*, my surname has always been the source of much merriment. Pronunciations include Fashlah, Feckler, Pichler, Fatchelor, Fletcher, and a few others that I leave to the reader's imagination. Once, in West Cork, I was introduced to an audience as Yanky Faulkner.

My surname was the cause of a memorable first day at school for my older son Ashi. When the teacher read the roll, she mispronounced Fachler. Ashi informed her of the right pronunciation. A couple of hours later, she again mispronounced the name. Again he corrected her. The third time she did it, Ashi retorted, "Miss, you're stupid." His school career could only go downhill from there.

On my own first day in boarding school, I was accosted by, "Hey, new boy, what's your name?" In my innocence, I proudly informed him that it was Yanky Fachler. For some odd reason, he thought that both my first name and my second name were hilarious. He hastened to inform all his companions that Wanky Fuckler had arrived.

Since I understood neither the first nor the second cause of such merriment, I no idea what was so funny about either of the two mispronunciations. But I had enough presence of mind to decide on the spot that for the duration of my sojourn in boarding school, I would be Jack. And Jack I remained for the next seven years.

I remember hatching plans to change my name by deed-poll to Jack Thatch or James Fletcher (a pen-name that I have often used for writing magazine articles.)

But sticking with my name has paid dividends. There's no doubt that being the owner of a memorable (albeit unpronounceable) name is an advantage when you want to get noticed in the business world. A marketing guru once told me that I could never have invented a more unusual name if I'd tried.

The idea for a book that explores the nature of chutzpah popped into my head during the launch of my first book, **Fire in the Belly**. I had asked self-employed businessman Rodd Bond, the newly-installed president of my local Chamber of Commerce, to speak at the launch. He agreed, on condition that he could read the book first.

When Rodd went up to the podium to address the respectably-sized audience, I had no idea what he was going to say. He started with some complimentary comments about the book.

Then he said:

The chapter that really caught my attention and resonates with me is the chapter on chutzpah.

Even though he pronounced it like chutney, I knew at that moment that I wanted to write a book on chutzpah. And because, as Dershowitz says, chutzpah is best understood by its context, I started collecting chutzpah stories from various sources.

The heroes and heroines of these chutzpah stories all believed in the art of the impossible. They all chose unconventional routes to achieve their goals.

Chutzpah is not just used to describe people. Nowadays, products can have chutzpah too. *House & Home* magazine featured a heated bathroom towel rail "*that serves the same function as a plain radiator but with a bit more chutzpah.*"

Some of the chutzpah case studies in this book feature household-names like movie-maker Steven Spielberg, cartoon creator Walt Disney, rent-a-car maverick Warren Avis, and bagless vacuum cleaner inventor James Dyson.

Some of the chutzpah case studies feature people who might not be famous, but whose chutzpah inspired me. Other chutzpah stories I came across by chance.

For example, one evening I was enjoying a performance of Gilbert & Sullivan's *Trial By Jury*, staged in the Harry Ramsden's fish and chip restaurant in Belfast. I read a short paragraph about Harry on the menu, and asked the waitress if she could find any other material on him. The wad of information she gave me formed the basis for Harry's chutzpah story.

Several ideas for inclusion in this book were suggested by my California-based son Ashi (who was born with a chutzpah spoon in his mouth.) He would email me stories that he knew I would like.

I feel I should issue a word of caution about chutzpah. If you have ever looked up the word in an online or offline dictionary, you will also find several negative definitions, such as arrogance, impertinence and rudeness.

The famous Hans Christian Andersen tale of the Emperor's New Clothes provides examples of both negative and positive chutzpah.

The two rogues who appear at the court of a very vain emperor, claiming that they can weave a special garment that makes the wearer invisible to the stupid and the ignorant, represent the negative aspect of chutzpah.

The young boy who has the cheek to call everyone's bluff by calling out: "The emperor is naked!" (or, in the Danny

Kaye version, "The King is in the altogether, the altogether") is an example of positive chutzpah.

The confusion about the meaning of chutzpah can be traced back to the word's origin in the ancient 3,000-year-old language of Aramaic. Back then, chutzpah was not necessarily a positive trait. A person with chutzpah was someone who arrogantly and egotistically overstepped the boundaries of accepted polite behaviour. To this day, in modern Hebrew, being told that you have chutzpah is not necessarily a compliment.

However, the focus of this book is on the more modern – and more constructive – meaning of chutzpah.

All the true stories below elicited from me the same response: "What a chutzpah!" The pluck and panache of the individuals featured made me want to emulate their nerve.

I sincerely believe that we all have the chutzpah spark inside us, waiting to be allowed out.

I hope that the chutzpah stories below will encourage you to create your own chutzpah-inducing environment, a place where you can cultivate a wacky, non-conformist frame of mind.

Chapter 2

Thirty Centuries of Chutzpah

Imagine the scene. We are in Assyria some three thousand years ago. An artisan working on the stonework of a royal temple gets very tired in the mid-day sun. He approaches the taskmaster in charge of the project, and asks if he can take a rest.

"You've got some chutzpah coming to me and asking me that," barks the civil servant to the hapless artisan. But the words did not come out in English. They came out in Aramaic.

Aramaic once occupied the same prominence as English does today. It was the *lingua franca* of much of the Middle East, and was the language spoken by Jesus.

Aramaic was prominent for a period of about 1,500 years until the 7th century. It was the main language of the Persian, Babylonian and Assyrian empires, and spread as far as Greece and the Indus valley. Throughout these empires, Aramaic was a language of administration.

Aramaic belongs to the Semitic sub-family of the Afro-Asiatic language family and is still spoken by small communities in Iraq, Turkey, Iran, Armenia, Georgia and Syria. I wonder if the word chutzpah still pops up in their daily conversations.

At some point in time, the word chutzpah – together with thousands of other words – migrated to, and was fully absorbed by, its sister Semitic language, Hebrew.

A few hundred years ago, the word chutzpah migrated once more, this time from Hebrew to Yiddish, the Germano-Hebraic language spoken by Jews throughout Europe from the Middle Ages up to the last century. In Yiddish, chutzpah assumed a more benign meaning and was accompanied more with a smile than with a scowl. In Yiddish, a person with chutzpah was someone you admired as a gutsy non-conformist.

Towards the end of the 19th century, at about the time John Stuart Mill was bemoaning the lack of eccentricity in society, chutzpah made a further migration. This journey was across the Atlantic to New York, as part of the cultural baggage carried by the millions of Jewish refugees escaping the pogroms of Eastern Europe.

It was in America that chutzpah acquired an even more cheeky meaning, and started to make serious inroads into everyday language.

Yiddish words that have found their way into everyday language

Chutzpah is just one of the many Yiddish words that have entered the American mainstream. Other examples include:

- Shmooze: gossip, informal chitchat
- Mayven: an expert
- Mish-mash: hodgepodge
- Nu? : so?
- Nosh: snack
- Shmuck: jerk (also slang for the male organ)
- Spiel: promotional patter
- Tush: backside
- Kosher: above board, legitimate (literally: conforming to Jewish dietary laws)
- Kvetch: complain
- Schlep: to drag or haul something, to make a tedious journey
- Schmaltz: excessive sentimentality (literally: chicken fat)
- Shmutter: rag
- Shlemiel: clumsy dolt
- Shlemazel: the poor unfortunate on whose toes the shlemiel always drops heavy objects
- Oy: An expression of surprise, excitement, anger, anguish or anything else you would like it to mean.
- Oy gevalt: Oh heavens, Oh what will become of us?
- Kvetsch: complainer
- Nebech: nerd
- Kvell: to glow with pride
- Metziyeh: a bargain
- Schnorer: beggar

In *The Joys of Yiddish*, Leo Rosten describes chutzpah as a quintessentially arrogant word – because it refuses to be precisely translated. "No other word, and no other language, can do justice to it," writes Rosten.

Chutzpah is everywhere. You'll hear chutzpah used in the movies and on TV. You'll find horses, yachts, magazines and nightclubs called Chutzpah. There are websites that feature Chutzpah Awards. There's an annual Chutzpah Arts Festival in Canada. There's a Chutzpah Hall of Fame.

In the space of a couple of years, the number of chutzpah entries on Google has grown ten-fold to one and a half million. And talking of Google, some would describe Al Gore's boast that he was responsible for the widespread popularity of the Internet as a supreme example of sheer chutzpah.

Hamlet – edited, enlarged and improved by Joseph Kowalski

Nobel laureate and Yiddish writer Isaac Bashevitz Singer relates that as a young man in Poland, he paid a visit to the home of the famous writer, Joseph Kowalski.

The young Singer came across a Yiddish-language book with the title: "Hamlet - by William Shakespeare. Edited, Enlarged and Improved by Joseph Kowalski."

This, says Singer, is the definition of chutzpah.

Chutzpah may be difficult to translate, but it has no shortage of synonyms. In fact, I am considering submitting a claim to the *Guinness Book of Records*, in the sincere belief that I have gathered together in one place the largest number of chutzpah synonyms ever attempted (78 nouns, 37 adjectives).

Ladies and gentlemen, it gives me great pleasure to announce the maiden appearance of:

Yanky's Record-Breaking Chutzpah Synonym List

noun

1.	assumption	21.	courage
2.	attitude	22.	crust
3.	audaciousness	23.	dareness
4.	audacity	24.	daring
5.	balls	25.	daring do
6.	ballsiness	26.	derring do
7.	beitzim (Yiddish)	27.	effrontery
8.	boldness	28.	enthusiasm
9.	bollix (courtesy of Dave McArdle)	29.	exuberance
		30.	face
10.	bottle	31.	fearlessness
11.	brashness	32.	feistiness
12.	brass	33.	flair
13.	brass neck	34.	foolhardiness
14.	brazenness	35.	forwardness
15.	brio	36.	funkiness
16.	cheek	37.	gall
17.	cheekiness	38.	gumption
18.	cockiness	39.	gustiness
19.	cojones (Spanish)	40.	gusto
20.	confidence	41.	guts

42. hubris
43. impishness
44. impudence
45. ingenuity
46. irreverence
47. liveliness
48. mettle
49. moxie
50. neck
51. nerve
52. outrageousness
53. overconfidence
54. panache
55. passion
56. pertness
57. pith
58. pluck
59. pluckiness
60. presumption
61. presumptuous-ness
62. pushiness
63. quirkiness
64. rashness
65. sassiness
66. sauce
67. sauciness
68. self-confidence
69. shamelessness
70. smart-alecness (courtesy of Sarah Ingle)
71. spirit
72. spunk
73. temerity
74. verve
75. vitality
76. vivacity
77. wackiness
78. zeal

adjective

1. anarchistic
2. audacious
3. ballsy
4. bold
5. brash
6. brazen
7. cheeky
8. cocky
9. courageous
10. daring
11. exuberant
12. fearless
13. feisty
14. foolhardy
15. forward
16. funky
17. gutsy
18. impish
19. irreverent
20. madcap
21. maverick
22. mettlesome
23. off-the-wall
24. outrageous
25. pithy
26. plucky

27. presumptuous
28. quirky
29. sassy
30. saucy
31. self-confident
32. self-possessed

33. shameless
34. spirited
35. spunky
36. unabashed
37. wacky

The media has long had a love affair with the word chutzpah. It is a copywriter's delight. Take this headline that appeared in *Business Week*, for example: "Drive By Chutzpah in Silicon Valley." The article was about a New York entrepreneur who chose an unusual way to seek venture capital - displaying his own huge image on Silicon Valley billboards. Whoever wrote the *Business Week* headline assumed that business readers would be familiar with chutzpah.

When the *US School Library Journal* used a headline: "Five Librarians, One 50 foot Phone Cord, and a Whole Lot of Chutzpah," it too assumed that its librarian readers understand the term.

And when the London *Observer* wrote: "If the academic world gave degrees for chutzpah, the Massachusetts Institute of Technology would have a string of honorary doctorates," it assumed that its readership grasped the meaning of chutzpah.

But it's not just headline writers in the USA and UK who love to use the word. Chutzpah has become a global phenomenon. *Business Line* in India wrote: "You don't get to be the richest man in the world without a lot of chutzpah."

The Chutzpah Letter that Landed
Craig Smith in the West Wing

Traditionally, the kind of people who go and work in the White House as presidential speechwriters have given up careers as journalists, novelists, PR consultants or political activists.

Craig Smith's route to the White House was somewhat different.

Smith was a professor of communication studies, and was invited in 1976 to deliver a guest lecture at the University of North Carolina. While he was there, he went along to hear President Gerry Ford address the Future Homemakers of America.

Smith was appalled when the president totally ignored the feminism issue, and decided to write to Ford. He did not spare the president any criticism, describing Ford's performance as "embarrassing."

Smith never seriously imagined that his shrill letter would elicit a reply. To his surprise, he was summoned a few days later to Washington for an interview. He was invited to stay a week and evaluate all of Ford's speeches. When asked for his opinion of Ford's style, Smith replied: "He doesn't have one."

"If you think you can do better, show us," he was told – which is how Craig Smith became the longest serving speechwriter in the Ford Administration. And all because he sat down and wrote a chutzpah letter.

In the Philippines, the president campaigned on a ticket that he had the experience and expertise to lead the country out of its economic misery. Once in office, he asked the country's help in solving a financial crisis. This, said the *Manila Times*, was chutzpah.

> **A chutzpah headline is very, very sure of itself. A chutzpah headline has to appear bombastic, but quickly dissolve into a pleasant and rewarding discovery. The chutzpah headline isn't brash - it's pure, unadulterated charm.**
> *Dennis Altman, professor of advertising and PR, University of Kentucky*

The word chutzpah appears in headlines of the English-language *Russian Journal*, *Environment Hawaii*, and even the English-language edition of Egypt's *Al-Ahram*.

The extent to which chutzpah can be said to have become truly global is evident from the fact that it has entered the lexicon of Saudi Arabia's Prince Bandar Bin Sultan. Commenting on the demand of countries that opposed the war in Iraq to secure reconstruction contracts, he said: "It just takes so much chutzpah."

It can't have been too difficult for Irish readers to understand the headline in the *Irish Examiner*. "If prizes were handed out for sheer chutzpah, Ryanair would scoop the pool."

In a similar vein, readers of Ireland's *Fingal Independent* could have grasped something of the word's meaning from the headline: "Plenty of chutzpah is the key to solid business brain." (In all fairness, I should point out that this particular article featured a seminar conducted by corporate trainer, Yanky Fachler!)

Catch a Train to Catch Your Target

The story so far ...

In 1945, just after the end of WW2, it was not universally apparent that the market was ready for a colour magazine targeted at African-American readers. So it was a leap of faith that led John H Johnson to launch *Ebony*, which he promoted as a kind of *Life* magazine for the African-American market.

Johnson knew that the long-term survival of his magazine depended on persuading white ad agencies to buy space in his new magazine. So he started sending letters and placing calls to corporate chiefs and the heads of ad agencies. Sometimes his efforts succeeded, but more often than not they did not. "It was hard getting through," he once said, "but I was fighting for my life, and I placed as many as 400 phone calls to the same CEO."

There was one particular quarry that Johnson was intent on contacting. If only he could meet this ad agency head, he could convince the man to steer ads in *Ebony*'s direction. But despite his best efforts, he simply could not pin the guy down.

The chutzpah moment

After doing his homework, Johnson discovered a curious fact about the ad agency head – he did not like flying. Which is why he travelled by train every Sunday afternoon from Chicago to New York. Armed with this critical piece of information, Johnson started travelling on the same train each Sunday. On every trip, he frequented the club car where the CEO dined. Casual nods eventually turned to friendly chats. Friendly chats eventually turned to an invitation to dine.

... and the consequences

Johnson's strategy worked a treat. He lost no opportunity in turning the dinner invitation to his advantage, and explained why he believed that *Ebony* was the ideal advertising vehicle for the ad agency's clients. The agency head agreed, and before long the ads were flowing to *Ebony*. Johnson went on to become the first African American to attain major success in magazine and book publishing.

Here are some more examples of how headline writers and feature writers use chutzpah in their newspapers and magazines:

- *New York Times*: "Senator Describes Commuter Tax as Legislative Chutzpah."
- *Washington Post*: "From Russia With Chutzpah."
- *Reuters*: "Nashville Learns The Meaning Of Chutzpah."
- *TheStreet.com*: "With a Little Chutzpah and a Lot of Faith, Via Takes on Intel."

- *Information Week*: "Chutzpah May Be Missing Coin in Salary Negotiations."
- *Irish Independent*: "You have to admire his chutzpah in getting published."
- *Sunday Tribune*: "Nagle shows chutzpah."

How does the business media define chutzpah?

- *The Economist*: that upbeat sense of self-confidence that says anything is possible, go for it, and never be too shy to ask for help.
- *Entrepreneur* magazine: daring to dream, facing fears, taking risks, finding balance, giving back, growing new eyes and laughing at life.
- Donald Trump claimed that the winner of his *The Apprentice* reality TV show had to have intelligence, chutzpah and street-smarts.
- *Inc.com*: By dint of ingenuity, doggedness and chutzpah, it is still possible to bootstrap a company – and thrive.

**The single biggest reason most businesses fail
is the lack of chutzpah when needed.
Successful business owners all share a healthy
cynicism, insecurity and chutzpah.**
Cliff Ennico

Owners Posing as Salesmen

The story so far ...

Don Winter, Michael Travin and Larry Gelfand invested $1,000 of their own money in a controlled-circulation community newspaper for New York's Upper East Side. The first thing they needed was a mock-up of the tabloid, which they intended to show to retailers in an effort to secure prepaid advertising.

The trio spend half their investment in producing the mock-up, but it was a disaster. They couldn't use it, and they were left with nothing to show potential advertisers. With little option, the three founders were forced to try and solicit advertising without a mock-up. To complicate matters, they also realised that if they offered payment terms of 30 or 60 days, they would not be able to fund their paper.

The chutzpah moment

The only solution was to make sure they walked out of a sales call with cash. And the only way to do this was to appear as if they represented a fat, happy company run by smooth professionals. They hoped that by creating the illusion that they were part of a larger group, they would inspire confidence in advertisers who would have felt much less comfortable giving money to a new untried start-up.

Don, Michael and Larry presented themselves as salesmen, not the owners. They acted like three cogs in a reassuringly larger machine. Their business cards described them as account executives, and they always introduced themselves as sales reps.

... and the consequences

Their tactic worked. Within three months, they had sold thousands of dollars worth of advertising – for cash.

They used the same ploy with printers. By projecting an image of an established company, they managed to secure 30 days credit. As unknown first-time customers, they could never have obtained such favourable terms.

Imagine that you are the founder of a multi-million dollar lingerie company. Imagine that you are determined to get on to a popular TV chat show. And imagine that after several rebuffs, you finally receive the hallowed invitation.

Are you filled with gratitude, or do you start making demands that could give the show's producer's second thoughts?

Tiffany James, president of UndercoverWear, was no stranger to TV. She had appeared on dozens of channels. But despite her popularity, she was not able to persuade the producers of the one show she really wanted, Donahue, to invite her. She did not give up. She secured an appearance on *Evening Magazine*, and sent an unsigned cable to Donahue's home saying simply: Watch *Evening News* tonight.

He did, and the very next day, she was invited to appear on *Donahue*. But before she appeared on the show, Tiffany had conditions. Lots of conditions. When she was offered a 13-minute slot, she turned it down. It had to be the full hour, or nothing. When the producers upped their offer to 30 minutes, Tiffany still adamantly refused to compromise. A full hour or nothing.

Eventually they gave in, but Tiffany had another chutzpah ace up her sleeve. Actually, it was on her head. She had the nerve to wear her hair in the same way that Donahue's wife always wore hers. Donahue was totally bowled over by this dynamic businesswoman, and UndercoverWear achieved an audience of millions. No surprises for guessing which lingerie company saw its sales go through the roof.

Selling a Domain Name to Afford UN membership

The story so far ...

Internet Corporation for Assigned Names & Numbers (ICANN) is the international organisation responsible for building and sustaining the global Internet, and for co-ordinating the management of domain names. ICANN hands out country-code top level domains, known in technical jargon as ccTLDs. For example, Turkmenistan was assigned .tm, and the Federation of Micronesia in the South Pacific was assigned .fm.

When Jason Chapnik learned that the domain name of the tiny Micronesian island of Tuvalu (population: 10,000) was .tv, he spotted a business opportunity. Chapnik was convinced that he could profitably provide Internet-savvy companies with the chance of branding their websites with one of the most recognized two-letter combinations in the world.

The chutzpah moment

Chapnik approached the authorities of Micronesia, and in a bidding war, he offered to buy the exclusive right to use the .tv domain for $60 million over a 10 year period. The islanders could not believe their luck. At the time, there were no Internet connections on the island, and no dotcom boom. The $20 million downpayment represented double Tuvalu's annual GDP. Naturally, the islanders agreed, and sold Chapnik the rights to the .tv domain name.

... and the consequences

Chapnik's chutzpah worked. The .tv domain name fast became highly sought after, and more than 70,000 TV stations, shows and channels have already signed up. The windfall for Tuvalu allowed the island to finally afford the registration fee for joining the United Nations.

When you look back at the case studies in this chapter, ask yourself what is preventing you from sending a letter to the White House like Craig Smith did.

Couldn't you have come up with the stunt that John H Johnson pulled to beef up the advertising revenue of his magazine?

Were Don, Michael and Larry the only people in the world who could have thought of using creative chutzpah to solve their problem?

Do you have to be a Tiffany James to make impossible demands instead of showing how grateful you are?

And, assuming you had the money to start with, is there any reason why you could not have come up with the same idea as Chapnik?

The answer to all these questions is a resounding No! It wasn't university degrees, technical qualifications, or special potions that allowed them to do what they did. It was simply a matter of letting the chutzpah genie out of the bottle.

And everyone can do that.

Chapter 3

"Go easy on me,
I'm an orphan"

Chutzpah and the law enjoy an interesting relationship. Most websites and Yiddish anthologies illustrate the meaning of chutzpah by telling the story of the young man found guilty of murdering both his parents.

When it comes to sentencing, he pleads clemency from the court. "On what grounds?" asks the judge. "On the grounds that I'm an orphan," replies the accused.

That's chutzpah.

Some jurists claim, only partly in jest, that Latin is being replaced by Yiddish as the spice in American legal argot. Whenever the English language fails to provide a proper alternative, Yiddish is happy to step into the breach. Among the Yiddish words that have appeared in court rulings are *kibitzer* (someone who wisecracks) and *klutz* (a blockheaded bungler).

The first time that chutzpah is reported in the US courts was in 1972, in an opinion of the Georgia Court of

Appeals. Since then, the Seventh Circuit has acknowledged that words like chutzpah have become absorbed into standard English and are now applied to members of all racial and ethnic groups. The Court of Federal Claims runs a Chutzpah Championship, the D.C. Circuit has a Chutzpah Award, and the Federal Circuit has a Chutzpah Doctrine.

There is a classic chutzpah story of the man who goes to a lawyer.

"How much do you charge for legal advice?" he asks the lawyer.

"A thousand dollars for three questions."

"Wow! Isn't that kind of expensive?"

"Yes, it is. What's your third question?"

In a case before an American court, the judge wrote: "It takes a particularly high degree of chutzpah ... to contradict this proposition." Significantly, the same judge felt the need to quote the *American Heritage Dictionary* definition of the words "decency" and "respect". But he felt no need to define the term "chutzpah" in his decision!

A federal district court in Washington noted that chutzpah is "presumption-plus-arrogance such as no other word, and no other language can do justice to". A federal court in the Northern District of Illinois defined chutzpah as audacity, impudence and brass. A New

Jersey court stated that "legal chutzpah is not always undesirable, and without it our system of jurisprudence would suffer". One judge recently described the attitude of a certain government action as "mega-chutzpah".

When Women Were Not Allowed to Be in Business on Their Own

The story so far ...
Today, the idea that a woman can be a successful lawyer is unremarkable. But back in the fifties in the USA, it was not easy for a woman to become a lawyer. In the state of Texas, it was almost impossible.

After studying at night for five years, Louise Raggio graduated as the only woman student from Southern Methodist University's Law School class of 1952. She was a single parent, and raised her three sons alone. Louise made the unpleasant discovery that despite her qualifications, there was not a law firm in Dallas that would hire her. At that time, women were simply not welcome in law firms, unless they were there to type, file and make coffee.

Left with little choice, Louise decided to open her own law practice at home, and made her living writing wills for $15 a piece. But she found herself in a Catch-22 situation. A married woman's signature was not legally binding in Texas. In other words, without a husband's signature, Louise could not get a bank loan or sign a bail bond.

The chutzpah moment

An outraged Louise decided to have the law changed.
Fuelled by her determination to combat the inequality of
women in business, she directed a task force in the mid-
1960s that resulted in the Texas Marital Property Act
of 1967, which gave married women in Texas the right to
conduct business and control property.

... and the consequences

Louise's victory in Texas ultimately helped pave the way
for women all over the country to become entrepreneurs.
Not content with changing state law, Louise and a group
of women lawyers then successfully sued banks, airlines,
and accounting and law firms on charges of sex
discrimination. Again, thanks to her efforts, doors were
opened for the first time to women in many new
professions.

Louise Raggio, the woman who rewrote the law, was
among fifteen influential entrepreneurs named to
Fortune Small Business magazine's first Hall of Fame.

A misinterpretation of the word chutzpah has even led to
litigation. When Senator Charles Schumer said of
someone: "In Brooklyn, we have a word for something like
that - chutzpah," the senator was unsuccessfully sued
for making false and defamatory statements! Someone
obviously did not understand that Schumer was not being
offensive.

The US Internal Revenue Service had to clamp down on
so-called Chutzpah Trusts - a clever tax avoidance

scheme based on complicated borrowing and forward-sales-contract techniques.

A recent example of legal chutzpah was the case of Wesley Fitzpatrick in Kansas City. Fitzpatrick was granted a temporary restraining order against a female who he said was stalking him, claiming in court that he had become "scared, depressed and in fear for my freedom". When the judge discovered that the stalker was actually Fitzpatrick's parole officer, he decided to rescind the restraining order.

Getting into the Movies in order to Become a Lawyer

Barbara Olson thought she wanted to be a teacher. After completing high school, she completed a teaching degree from college. It was only then that she realised that what she really wanted was to become a lawyer.

The decision to study law was easy. Finding the funds to afford pay for college was not. Barbara had to raise $50,000 to make her law dream come true, but her options were very limited. Yes, she could always teach. After all, she did have a respectable teaching degree. But Barbara worked out that that by the time she saved the $50,000 on a teacher's salary, she would be too old to practice law anyway. So she started looking for a job that paid well but that did not require a special degree. The somewhat unlikely destination that she chose was Hollywood. She called hundreds of production companies, asking for a job.

When she was asked about her previous experience, Barbara was deliberately vague. She did manage to give the impression that she had experience in TV. She neglected to volunteer the information that this experience was limited to a single show that she worked on while at college.

Eventually, a movie production company gave Barbara a job as a bookkeeper and associate producer. Over the next six years, she worked in several production companies until she had saved her $50,000. As soon as she reached her target, she quit the movie business. Aware that to stay in Hollywood was to tempt fate, she looked around for a law school that was commencing immediately – and promptly enrolled.

Barbara proved that necessity is the mother of chutzpah. She talked her way into the movie business because she needed the money to fund her law studies. And once she graduated with her law degree, she went on to enjoy a highly lucrative and influential career as an attorney and conservative commentator.

My first direct encounter with the law was when I was six years old. I found a penny in the street, and was encouraged by my mother to take it to the local police station. The officer on duty duly made a report, and told me that if no one claimed the penny within three months, it was mine. Sure enough, three months later, I received a postcard from the police station informing me that I could come in and claim the unclaimed penny.

Round about this time, my father had dealings of his own with the law. Eli Fachler saw that his dead-end job in a local butcher shop was going nowhere, and he heard that a small wholesale wine business was for sale. He borrowed some money from a cousin and bought the business.

A friendly wine importer who was impressed with Eli's enthusiasm, agreed to grant him generous payment terms that would provide him with the working capital he needed. Eli left the butcher shop and opened the Hadassah Wine Company.

Under British law at the time, a wholesale business did not require a license. But Eli saw that the real profits lay in opening a retail wine shop on the same premises. This meant going to the courts to obtain a retail license. Everyone advised Eli to get a local solicitor to handle the application in the Magistrates Court. The lazy solicitor failed to anticipate that a cartel of local licensed trade interests would oppose the application and, on the day, Eli's request for a retail license was dismissed.

The application should have been a formality. Now Eli was stuck without the retail license he so desired. He would have to reapply, but who could guarantee that his next application would succeed?

Ignoring everyone's advice, Eli decided to handle the next application alone, with no legal representation. Instead of trying to fight the objections of the trade, as his legal team would have suggested, Eli chose another route altogether. He had postcards printed with the following wording:

"I the undersigned feel that there is a need for a
local wine shop, and I therefore support the
application of Mr. Eli Fachler for a retail license."

I still remember helping to stick the stamps on the
postcards, which were distributed to every household in
a 500-yard radius of the premises. To ensure that the
postcards were delivered to every household, Eli enlisted
the help of the local Boy Scouts group. These eager Bob-
a-Job youngsters diligently distributed the postcards,
and dozens of postcards soon came cascading through
our letterbox every single day.

Eli attended the next licensing session of the
Magistrates Court with his bundle of postcards. The
bemused magistrates had never seen such chutzpah. Not
only was an applicant appearing without legal
representation, but the applicant had taken the unheard-
of step of canvassing support from local residents.

The magistrates were so impressed that they took the
unusual decision to override the objections from the
trade. They threw out the earlier dismissal, and granted
my dad his retail license.

The Unofficial Beer of the
2002 Winter Olympics

Imagine that you live in the teetotal Utah, where 70% of the residents are Mormons who frown upon alcohol consumption. Imagine that you go against all logic and open the first brewery in Utah for more than 20 years.

Any normal person would keep his head down. But Greg Schirf was no ordinary person. In 1986, he founded the Wasatch Brewery in Park City, and from the very start, he managed to land himself in legal entanglements.

When he first opened his brewery, he gave away free beer to the community by way of celebration. When this turned out to be illegal, he found a loophole in an arcane Utah law, and opened the state's first brewpub.

In July 1998, with the 2002 Olympic Winter Games in Salt Lake City on the horizon, Schirf knew that tiny Wasatch could not afford to become an official sponsor. However, he did want to cash in on the Games. His cheeky strategy was the slogan: "Wasatch - The Unofficial Beer of the 2002 Winter Games".

The US Olympic Committee (USOC), the Salt Lake Organizing Committee (SLOC), and Anheuser-Busch, the official Olympic beer sponsor, were not amused. But when SLOC sent Schirf a cease-and-desist order, he ran to the local media to complain he was getting picked on.

Schirf next got into trouble with his "The Other Local Religion, Wasatch Beers. Baptise your taste buds" slogan. A radio spot featured two "missionaries" on a door-to-door campaign seeking Wasatch converts. Schirf's tactics again caused mayhem, with every talkshow on radio discussing the campaign.

The last straw was when Schirf renamed one of his beers Polygamy Porter (tag line: "Why have just one?"). The Utah Alcoholic Beverage Control Commission declared a ban on using religious themes in alcohol advertising.

But by now, Schirf had attracted not just the local media but the international media too. The *Economist*, the Associated Press, and the BBC all featured the local controversy. The story of the billboard controversy won the attention of beer distributors in other states, and Schirf's Utah Brewers Cooperative soon held over half of the microbrew market in Utah.

There is a true story of a California bank robber who had just sprinted out the door of California Savings & Loan in Oakland when the booby-trapped bundle of cash he had stuffed into his pocket exploded. The explosion caused second- and third-degree burns around the thief's genitals. After being sentenced to eight years, the thief had the chutzpah to file a lawsuit claiming that his injuries entitled him to $2 million in damages, on the grounds that the punishment for bank robbery is not maiming.

The story is also told of the old man who joins the end of a long line of people waiting for the bus. He holds his hand to his chest, taps the shoulder of the woman in front of him, and says: "If you had what I've got, you'd let me in front of you." She yields up her place in the line, and the old man repeats this until he finds himself at the front of the line. It's very hot on the bus, and the old man sees a girl take out a fan and start fanning herself. He says to her, "If you had what I've got, you would give me that fan." The girl gives him the fan. In between stops, the man tells the driver he wants to get off. The driver tells him he has to drop him at the next corner, not in the middle of the block. With his hand across his chest, the old man tells the driver, "If you had what I've got, you would let me off the bus right here." The bus driver pulls over immediately, and as the old man is about to get out, the driver asks him, "Sir, what is it you have?" The old man looks at him and nonchalantly replies, "Chutzpah."

The First Legal Brewery Pub since Prohibition

The story so far …

Bert Grant was born in Dundee, Scotland. Raised in Canada, he went to work as a young man in Yakima, Washington State, USA. He started working in the brewing industry when he was 16. Within three decades, Grant had established an international reputation as a highly-knowledgeable beer consultant.

He had always believed that the secret of good beer lay in the hops, and he planned to use the hops that grew in Yakima to produce a beer that would prove more flavourful than other beers on the market.

Putting his money where his taste buds were, Grant converted a 19th century former opera house, and created the Yakima Brewing & Malting Company microbrewery, using only locally-grown hops.

Within a very short time, Yakima beer started to attract
devotees. From just a few kegs of the Yakima beer,
Grant watched his idea blossom. As word spread, more
and more people were flocking to his brewery from far
and wide to sample his beer.

The chutzpah moment

The trouble began when Grant felt he owed it to his
visitors to enhance their comfort by installing a few
chairs in the lobby of the brewery. This simple gesture
came to the attention of the Washington licensing
officials, who decided that this was against the law.

They descended on the Yakima microbrewery like a
plague of locusts, and proceeded to do what officious
officials the world over do best – they hounded him.
They informed Grant that he couldn't serve beer on his
premises because he didn't have a license.

But Bert had not installed his seats without doing his
research. He pointed the officials to a little-known
loophole in the law which allowed every brewer to
operate one pub on the premises.

... and the consequences

The licensing officials had obviously not done their
homework, and were forced to concede. Grant's Brewery
Pub became the very first legal brewery pub in the whole
United States since Prohibition.

Thanks to Bert's determination and chutzpah, Yakima
went on to become one of the leading microbusinesses in
the Northwest.

Professor Alan Dershowitz illustrates chutzpah by describing examples from his own clients. One man, who was convicted of selling false antiques, tried to pay his legal fees to Dershowitz in antiques. When Dershowitz helped another client win her criminal case, she sued him for malpractice on the grounds that she was now unable to continue to defraud the government.

Arrest me, please!

An example of chutzpah in the courtroom was the case of British mother-of-three Julie Amiri, a serial shoplifter who claimed that she had orgasms every time she was detained by police or security guards.

Whenever Mrs Amiri appeared in court on charges of shoplifting in Oxford Street, she had the same excuse: "I stole in order to get arrested in order to have an orgasm."

The amazing thing is that Mrs Amiri persuaded doctors that her condition was genuine. Despite more than 50 arrests for shoplifting, she was never once convicted.

Chutzpah has even reached the hallowed corridors of one of the world's oldest law-making bodies, the House of Commons in London, the "Mother of Parliaments". Commenting on the proposal that Northern Ireland's Westminster MPs should have the right to speak in the Irish Parliament on issues relating to the peace process, one British MP said: "There is a word for this idea ... Chutzpah."

If you found yourself in Louise Raggio's situation, and discovered that a married woman's signature is not legally binding without your husband's signature, wouldn't your anger encourage you to turn to chutzpah for a solution?

If you were trying to get into the movies in order to raise $50,000 for your law school fees, mightn't you tempted to be deliberately vague about your previous experience like Barbara Olson?

If you were thwarted in your efforts to obtain a retail wine license, couldn't you have come up with Eli Fachler's idea of getting round trade objections by galvanising support from the local residents?

Admittedly, Greg Schirf has a particular penchant for chutzpah-fuelled marketing stunts. But couldn't you also think of attention-grabbing ways of promoting your business?

If over-zealous licensing officials tried to close you down on a technicality, couldn't you have followed Bert Grant's example and found a legal loophole that allowed you to open the very first legal brewery pub in the whole United States since Prohibition?

I'm convinced that you could. I'm convinced that we all have the capacity to produce chutzpah solutions. We just need to allow our imaginations to soar a little higher.

Chapter 4

Showbiz Chutzpah

You have to have a few screws loose to think
you can compete against the multibillion-dollar
giants. What's more, it takes chutzpah to do
it with little money.
Bob Weinstein

Chutzpah and showbiz are natural partners. An obituary
of actress Anne Bancroft concluded with the words: "In
all her efforts, Bancroft demonstrated equal measures
of chutzpah and grace."

When asked by a theatre director to make some changes
to the script (his own), Oscar Wilde had the chutzpah to
reply: "Who am I to tamper with a masterpiece?"

Reviewing a performance of Gershwin's *Porgy & Bess*, one
critic wrote:

> *Gershwin is sometimes portrayed as little more than a
> Tin Pan Alley tunesmith who had the temerity (perhaps
> the Yiddish word chutzpah is more appropriate) to
> intrude into the realm of serious music.*

Film producer Jerry Weintraub was attempting to tempt Julia Roberts to appear in his movie *Ocean's Eleven*. It was common knowledge that at the time, she was able to command $20 million per movie. Weintraub is reported to have sent her a $20 bill with an attached note: "We hear you get 20 a picture".

Oprah's Chutzpah Awards

Oprah Winfrey has long discovered the importance of chutzpah. On her website, she describes the attributes of the women who have been chosen to receive the Oprah Chutzpah Awards:

"These women have pushed, pulled, prodded, and persevered through thick and thin, poverty and wealth, hope and hopelessness, past naysayers and yes-men. Meet nine women whose chutzpah – audacity, nerve, boldness, conviction – has taken them to the most amazing places."

An example of on-screen chutzpah appears in the 1983 movie *The Scarlet & the Black*. The plot of the movie tells of Monsignor Hugh O'Flaherty (Gregory Peck), an Irish priest based in the Vatican who helps the Italian anti-Nazi resistance. In one memorable scene, a British soldier disguised as an Italian peasant, manages to get the German military commander of Rome to give him his autograph.

The reason why this example of chutzpah has special resonance for me is that this scene is based on a true-life incident involving my late friend and mentor, John Furman. Before he became a prominent businessman and public figure, and before the two of us founded Israel's national amateur drama association, John was a decorated captain with the British Army during WW2.

As John relates in his autobiography, *Be Not Fearful*, he was captured several times by the Germans and the Italians, but always managed to find an audacious way of escaping. He eventually made his way to Nazi-occupied Rome, where he joined a group which included O'Flaherty in running an elaborate underground escape route for Allied airmen.

John had always been a keen opera lover, and he did not believe that war should disturb his cultural pursuits. Dressed like a peasant, and without speaking a word of Italian, he loved nothing better than to frequent the opera in Rome.

One evening, John spotted General Malzer, the Nazi Commander in Chief of Rome, in the foyer of the Opera House. Without batting an eyelid, John went up to him with his programme and indicated that he would like the general's autograph. General Malzer promptly obliged.

Hollywood's Chutzpah Whizzkid

The story so far ...

Steven Spielberg is the genius behind some of the most memorable, award-winning and top-grossing movies of all time, including *Jaws* (the first-ever $100 million mega-hit), *Close Encounters of the Third Kind* (my favourite movie), *Raiders of the Lost Ark*, and others.

After graduating from high school, Spielberg applied to study film at the University of Southern California Cinema School. Despite his obvious talents in film-making – he had been making movies since he was 8 years old – inexplicably, his application was turned down on two separate occasions.

Therefore, he decided to go with his second choice, and he enrolled in California State University in Long Beach to study English. But Spielberg's appetite for the world of the movies remained undiminished and unfulfilled, and he never gave up his plan to get a foothold in the movie business.

The chutzpah moment

While on a bus tour of Universal Studios, whether pre-planned or spontaneously, Spielberg's chutzpah got the better of him and he jumped off the bus.

As he wandered around the back lots, he discovered and commandeered an abandoned janitor's cabin, which he turned into his office.

He put his name on the door, and he had business cards printed saying "Steven Spielberg, Director".

> ### ... and the consequences
>
> Exchanging his trademark T-shirt and jeans for his more serious-looking Bar Mitzvah suit and tie, Spielberg would cheerfully greet the security guards by name every time he saw them. They got used to seeing him walking about with his clipboard, assumed he worked there, and waved him through.
>
> He befriended an editor who showed him a few things about filmmaking, and started production on *Amblin*, a short movie made with a $15,000 budget provided by a friend. When *Amblin* won several film festival awards, including a showing at the Atlanta Film Festival in 1969, Spielberg's career as a professional moviemaker took off. Universal's Television Division offered him a seven-year contract and, at the age of 23, Spielberg became the youngest director ever to be signed to a long-term deal with a major Hollywood studio. Spielberg's chutzpah earned him the nickname "Hollywood's chutzpah whizzkid."

When I was in my early thirties, I discovered the world of amateur dramatics. I hadn't been on stage since I participated in school productions (people still speak in hushed tones of my performance as the lion in George Bernard Shaw's *Androcles & the Lion*.)

I enjoyed "treading the boards", but I was soon equally attracted by the organisational aspect of belonging to a drama group. I started getting involved in promoting the performances, I started organising drama festivals, and eventually I served for several years on the executive board of the Tallinn-based International Amateur Theatre Association (also known as IATA, not to be confused with the International Air Travel Association.)

That is why I can so identify with the story of Judy Cramer. After graduating from the Guildhall School of Music, Judy spent some time on the stage. However, she discovered that she actually preferred to work behind the scenes, and she got a job as assistant to producer Tim Rice.

It was while working with Tim that Judy met Bjorn Ulvaeus and Benny Andersson, formerly of the Swedish pop group Abba, who were collaborating with Tim on the musical *Chess*. Abba had famously won the 1972 Eurovision Song Contest, and had dominated the pop charts with a string of hits. However, by the 1990s, the group had long since split up. Their music was regarded as passé.

Although Judy had never been an Abba fan before, her acquaintance with Bjorn and Benny got her hooked on their music. She got it into her head to make a film that told the Abba story through their songs. As she worked her way through various jobs in the film and TV industry over the next 10 years, Judy never gave up her idea, which had now evolved into a stage musical rather than a movie.

Encouraged by the agreement of Bjorn and Benny to consider giving her the rights to their songs if she could come up with a good enough story line, Judy decided to take the plunge. She gave up her job, and sought help in writing the script. This was risky, because Judy still had no guarantee that she would get the rights. Within a couple of years, Judy's money had run out. Her expenses had included lawyers' fees, flights around the world for meetings, and hiring a creative team. She had an overdraft of £20,000, and she had to sell her apartment.

Judy's belief in her idea gave her the strength to withstand pressure from her friends, who thought she was crazy and obsessed. With everyone trying to dissuade her from getting involved in a project that was doomed to failure, Judy hung in there. Her chutzpah paid off when she finally secured the rights from Bjorn and Benny. Together with them, she formed a company that held the rights to *Mamma Mia*. Judy even convinced Polygram, Abba's record producer, to put up £3 million, and Bjorn and Benny persuaded a Swedish bank to put up the rest.

Mamma Mia opened in April 1999, and was an instant smash hit. It has already grossed over $2 billion, and been seen in more than 80 cities by over 20 million people. Judy has no doubt that the secret of her success was sheer determination to make it happen: "You have to make people believe in what you are doing. It has taken every fibre of my focus and concentration".

Stick To What You Know, Mr Disney

The story so far ...

There can be very few people on Planet Earth who have not heard of Walt Disney. The cartoon empire that he founded has been giving pleasure to generations of kids and their parents for some 80 years. By the early 1950s, Disney was already head of a highly successful studio, and his creations were household names around the world.

One day, Disney got it into his mind that he wanted to create a big family park where parents and children could have fun together in the company of life-size Walt Disney characters. He commissioned the Stanford Research Institute to conduct a study on the ideal setting for his family park, and he bought 60 acres of orange groves in Anaheim, 25 miles south of Los Angeles, near the Santa Ana Freeway.

Finding eager partners willing to bankroll this venture proved much harder than he imagined. Disney's first shock came when his own studio was reluctant to come up with the funds. With little choice, Disney went to his bank.

His appearance in the bank was greeted with whoops of delight from the staff, who all loved the magic of Disney. But when he sat down with the bank manager and showed him his plans, the manager looked at him and said: "Mr Disney. You are the greatest animator the world has ever known. Your characters are part of our childhood, and part of our children's childhood. My advice to you is to stick to movies, Mr Disney. Don't go chasing some hare-brained scheme about which you know nothing".

The chutzpah moment(s)

Disney refused to take "No" for an answer, even though the next bank he approached had the same message. And the next. And the next. One hundred banks turned Disney down flat. Two hundred banks. Three hundred banks. Each time, the same story. After each refusal, Disney would arrange to meet another bank.

At any stage in his quest for funding, Disney could have given up. He could have persuaded himself that his vision was wrong. But his brand of stubborn chutzpah would not allow him to give up on idea that he knew was right.

... and the consequences

It was not until Walt Disney walked into the 330th bank that the manager interrupted him, and asked: "How much do you want, Mr. Disney?".

Disneyland opened in 1955, complete with live television coverage. The world's first theme park was an instant success, a success that was mirrored by Disneyworld in Orlando, Florida, 16 years later.

Imagine that you have written a musical score that you believe should be on the West End stage. Naturally, you need some big-name producer to adopt your idea. What do you do? Naturally, you try and track down Tim Rice.

Composer Stuart Brayson was certain that his musical version of *From Here to Eternity*, the classic movie based on the James Jones novel about American soldiers in Hawaii before Pearl Harbour, was a hit. He was equally certain that Tim Rice, who famously collaborated with

Andrew Lloyd Webber on hit musicals such as *Joseph &*
the Amazing Technicolor Dreamcoat and *Evita,* was his
passport to fame and fortune.

When all conventional methods of contacting Rice failed,
Brayson mustered up his chutzpah, and literally threw
the manuscript into Rice's car at a moment when the car
door was open.

A bemused Rice decided to read the manuscript, and
later declared it to be "the most exciting musical I have
heard in 20 years written by a new composer".

Rice was so impressed with the script that he agreed to
become associate producer for the West End musical
version.

If you obey all the rules, you miss all the fun.
Katherine Hepburn

Ben and Sandra are two highly-talented friends of mine
who live in New Jersey. Over the years, I've watched
them both perform on stage many times, and I know just
how they can captivate an audience. Some years back, the
Children's Theatre Centre of New Jersey that they had
founded was looking for suitable material that would
allow them to make a breakthrough into the schools
market. They knew they had to come up with something
that did not yet exist in that market.

Then Ben remembered that some years earlier, he had
written some fun material to help his young daughter

overcome her problems with maths at school. At the time, he had toyed with the idea of publishing this material in book form for other kids experiencing maths problems. Sandra had even come up with an amusing name for the book, *Arithmetickles*. The project had remained in a drawer ever since. "Why don't we do a maths show for kids in school," he said to Sandra. "I'll adapt some new material, I'll combine it with what I wrote, we'll have us a hit show."

"Sounds great," said Sandra. "But haven't you forgotten that you failed maths in high school." It was true. Ben had indeed driven his poor mother to distraction with his inability to grasp the basic rudimentaries of maths. How could someone who still felt traumatised by his own school experiences have the chutzpah to write a maths show and sell it to schools?

Since Ben's grasp of logic was as poor as his grasp of maths, he did not ponder too long over this philosophical question. He sat down and, in short order, he had written a one-man maths show based on theatre games, improvisations and fun activities. The response was phenomenal. Schools across the country lined up to book *Arithmetickles*. Demand was so great that Ben's theatre company had to take on two extra actors.

Five years later, Ben's maths show has already been produced in more than 1,500 schools to a total audience of over 350,000 students. After performing *Arithmetickles* at a major three-day convention of maths teachers, Ben was invited to dinner with the convention's organising committee. So there he was, Ben Bendor the maths dropout, sitting with 15 top maths educators and professors. When he was asked the inevitable question about how he thought up *Arithmetickles*, Ben did not have the heart to tell them the sad truth, so this is what he told them:

> "I used to be a really bad pupil, but in 5th grade my regular maths teacher was away for three months. It was the replacement teacher who changed my life. She used numerical magic tricks, games and competitions, and I so enjoyed playing with numbers and shapes that I lost my fear of maths. It was then that I knew that my mission in life was to help kids all over the world enjoy the beauty of maths."

The learned company had to wipe the tears from their eyes. So did I when I heard the story.

Make My Day

The story so far ...

When you are engaged in a fight for business, it is not always the most obvious weapons that win the battle.

This was certainly the case when Time Warner boss Steve Ross was engaged in a bidding war for Atari. Ross was determined to wow the Atari folk, in the hope that they would decide to sell their company to Time Warner rather than to a rival bidder.

Following protracted negotiations, it was agreed that Ross and his colleagues would conduct negotiations with the Atari executives in the Time Warner head office in New York City. Ross sent a company jet to San Jose to collect the Atari VIPs and bring them to the meeting.

Ross was determined to buy Atari, and he knew that in order to sway the Atari executives, he had to come up with a something really special, really different. In a masterstroke of lateral thinking, Ross decided to use a secret resource that he believed would do the trick.

The chutzpah moment

When the Atari executives climbed aboard the Time Warner jet, they were told that they were being joined on the flight by another passenger. Naturally, the Atari people raised no objection, and assumed that the extra passenger would be an anonymous Time Warner executive.

It is not difficult to imagine the surprise of the Atari executives when they climbed the steps of the executive jet, when the person sitting there was none other than movie star Clint Eastwood.

In order to impress the Atari people, Ross had arranged for the Hollywood star to just "happen" to need a ride in order to reach a shoot on location. Just as Ross predicted, the Atari executives were totally star-struck, and succumbed to the glamour of being in the vicinity of the megastar. They never questioned why Time Warner needed to deliver Eastwood to the film set exactly when the jet was to take them to New York. And when the pilot apologised that he had to make an unscheduled stop to allow Eastwood to disembark, the executives were even more impressed.

There is no doubt that Eastwood "made their day".

... and the consequences

When the Atari executives arrived in New York, they were still mesmerised by the experience of encountering a Hollywood icon on their flight. In the subsequent negotiations, Ross was able to acquire Atari on behalf of Time Warner at a knock-down price. Ross's none-too-subtle chutzpah had done the trick.

Clint Eastwood also has a walk-on part in the story of J Peterman. When I worked as a copywriter, I was always on the lookout for copy with a difference. One of the best examples of copy I ever came across was the J Peterman catalogue. The style was so outrageously romantic that I laughed on every page.

At the time, I didn't know anything about the history of the company. I assumed from the copy that John Peterman spent his time sourcing exotic items of apparel around the world, and then sitting down and writing about them in his inimitable style. I discovered that this was not exactly the case.

After a stint as a baseball player for a Pittsburgh Pirates farm team and sales manager of an indoor plant fertilizer company, John Peterman ran his own sales management consultancy. One day, his travels brought him to Jackson Hole, Wyoming. On an impulse, he stepped into a store, and bought himself a duster, the long cowboy coat that Clint Eastwood used to wear in his spaghetti westerns.

Peterman could not ignore the fact that as he made his way through the airport, his duster was attracting a fair share of stares, with several people coming up to him to ask where he bought it. So he bought a small stock of coats, and sold them from his home in Lexington, Kentucky. He placed small ads in *The New Yorker* and the *Wall Street Journal*, and within a few months, his dusters were selling in cities all over the US.

Encouraged by his success, Peterman created his trademark J Peterman catalogue, which he called an *Owner's Manual*. The oblong shaped catalogue printed on heavy, high-quality paper, was unique in the marketplace. There were no photographs of the clothes, just watercolour or pen-and-ink sketches, accompanied by a flowery Hemingway-esque style prose to describe the items on sale. Most of the descriptions included the global adventures of J Peterman as he travelled widely to source his hard-to-find clothes.

At the height of J Peterman's success, his idiosyncratic catalogue was read by up to 40 million people, who liked to fantasise that they too had been swept romantically through some past that never existed.

Peterman's chutzpah was threefold. One, the idea of turning his wacky coat into a business. Two, the fact that he never personally travelled to most of the exotic places that the catalogue described. And three, the fact that he did not write the copy that appeared in his name. His colleague, New York wordsmith Donald Staley, was responsible for that.

J Peterman eventually became a $50 million company, and was parodied on TV, where John Peterman was the model for a character on Seinfeld. In the late 1990s, the company went bankrupt and, in an astonishing example of life imitating art, the actor who played Peterman in Seinfeld helped the real Peterman relaunch the company in 2001.

Let me ask you something.

If you found yourself living in a totalitarian regime, couldn't you, like John Furman, be tempted to have a little fun at the expense of the authorities?

If you had a passion for film-making, but were turned down by film school, couldn't you get into movies through the backdoor, like Steven Spielberg's requisitioning of a disused cabin at Universal Studios?

If you believed that the world was ready for an Abba musical, couldn't you have made huge sacrifices, like Judy Cramer did when she refused to give up until *Mamma Mia* took the world by storm?

If you believed that you had found a novel idea, couldn't you have followed Walt Disney's example and defied all the doubters before opening the world's first theme park?

If you believed that only Tim Rice could get your musical on to the West End stage, couldn't you have followed Stuart Brayson's example and tossed the manuscript into Rice's car?

If you had written *Arithmetickles*, a show to help kids overcome their math problems, even though you flunked math at school, couldn't you like Ben Bendor, bluff your way through an evening with a bunch of math professors?

If you were desperate to impress a potential business partner, couldn't you have taken a leaf out of Steve Ross's book and brought along megastar Clint Eastwood to wow the Atari folk? (Well, maybe not – but there's nothing to prevent you from coming up with an equally out-of-the-box idea to wow them.)

If you wanted to launch a clothes catalogue, couldn't you have followed John Peterman's example and created a unique tongue-in-cheek style that helped you stand out from the crowd?

Your ability to use your chutzpah is not related to your expertise in any particular field. Chutzpah is a mindset, a willingness to suspend the normal rules, an ability to laugh at yourself, to have fun, and to give fun to others who hear about your exploits.

Chapter 5

Publishing Chutzpah

As most people know, James Fenimore Cooper wrote the 19th century classic, *The Last of the Mohicans*, which has inspired millions with its tale of life in the frontier wilderness. Which is fine, except that confirmed New Yorker Cooper never in his life ventured anywhere near the frontier or near an Indian reservation. That's chutzpah.

Because publishing is a field that requires a lot of luck, it can take chutzpah to persevere when publishers and others don't appreciate your genius. George Orwell's *Animal Farm* was rejected by 23 publishers, including Faber & Faber. The editor who turned down *Animal Farm* was TS Eliot, who told Orwell that he doubted "whether this is the right point of view from which to criticise the political situation at the present time".

A similar fate befell children's author Theodor Geisel, better known as Dr Seuss, who was also rejected by 23 publishers. Close behind comes James Joyce's *The Dubliners* with 22 rejections, and *M.A.S.H.* with 21 rejections. Six publishers turned down Beatrix Potter's *The Tale of Peter Rabbit*.

Or take Lawrence Peter. Sixteen publishers rejected his book, *The Peter Principle*, about the rise of individuals to their levels of incompetence. He stubbornly refused to give up, and his book eventually became a global publishing phenomenon.

When Stephen R. Covey informed his father that instead of joining the family hotel and property empire, he intended to train leaders, his father repeated the old adage: "Those who can, do. Those who can't, teach". This negativity did not deter Covey, who went on to write the best-selling *The 7 Habits of Successful People*.

Before *The Guinness Book of Records* went on to become an international publishing phenomenon, Guinness's advertising agency scoffed at the company's plan to publish a book on superlatives as an amateurish and inaccurate idea that "would never catch on".

A former BBC news department journalist had his thriller manuscript rejected by a string of major publishers. WH Allen turned it down on the grounds of "No reader interest". Finally, Hutchinson agreed to take a chance on Frederick Forsyth's *The Day of the Jackal*.

A colleague of mine claims to have collected 70 rejection slips from publishers before he eventually started his own publishing company.

"I Know Your Retail Manager"

The story so far ...

Australian-born Wendy Pye was a go-getting divisional manager for the NZ News publishing group in New Zealand, and had pioneered sales of its children's books into the US.

One day, she was unceremoniously fired. At the age of 42, and after 22 years with the company, she was given five minutes to clear her desk and was then frog-marched out of the building.

Although Wendy had never previously considered going out on her own, her reaction was swift and decisive. Within 24 hours, fuelled by a heavy dose of adversity and a desire for revenge, she decided to start a rival educational publishing business.

Her first priority was to seek a $US 100,000 bank loan. Easier said than done. All the banks Wendy approached in New Zealand turned her down.

The chutzpah moment

In a moment of inspiration, Wendy remembered that while travelling business class on an internal flight in Australia (she always travelled business class for the networking opportunities), she had sat next to the new retail manager of Westpac Asia Bank.

She typed up a business plan at home on a borrowed typewriter, and sent it to Westpac, even though this merchant bank only lent large dollars to large corporates. She justified her writing to the bank on the grounds that she was acquaintances with the retail manager.

... and the consequences

When Wendy's letter reached Westpac's Monte Heaven, he was so stunned by her chutzpah that he invited her for an interview. He decided to give her the loan at a cheap rate usually reserved for the bank's biggest customers. He told Wendy that anyone who could front up like she had was bound to succeed.

Heaven's confidence was to prove fully justified. Wendy convinced her new customers to pay in advance, and she never needed to use the loan to fund her growing business. Instead, she invested the money, earning a better rate of return than the interest she was paying. She went on to become New Zealand's publishing queen and one of the country's most inspiring business success stories.

According to the law of averages, my own publishing history should have followed in the hallowed example of other writers whose manuscripts were rejected again and again. But, for a combination of reasons, my maiden effort to have myself published hit the jackpot.

For over 20 years, I had been a freelance copywriter, a wordsmith for hire, writing brochures, ads, newsletters and more latterly websites. One weekend, I received a call out of the blue from my good friend Alan Clark, the best PR person that Scotland has ever produced.

Alan reeled off a list of my qualifications: I'd been my own boss for over 20 years, I'd spent several years strutting the amateur stage, I worked in the field of marketing communications, I was instinctively enthusiastic, I was always happy addressing an audience, I liked the sound of my own voice, I was critical of boring presentations, my work had brought me into contact with thousands of small and medium-sized business owner/managers, and my work demanded that I produce a steady stream of original and creative ideas.

"While I don't disagree with your prognosis", I said to Alan on the phone, "but where is all this leading?"

"It's obvious", he replied. "You should be motivating people in business. Goodbye." And with that he hung up. 90 seconds tops.

Instead of calling Alan back and telling him where he could take his crazy ideas, I allowed his suggestion to percolate inside my brain over the next 24 hours. Then I sat and wrote an outline for an entrepreneurial training module, based on the emotional transition from employee to self-employed. I was not overly concerned that I had never actually designed a training module before.

The next day, I contacted my local County Enterprise Board. I told them that I was an expert on entrepreneurship, and I explained why I thought I had something original to add to the field of business start-up training. I proposed that they adopt my "Do I Have What It Takes?" module as part of a programme targeted at people thinking of starting their own business.

Within days of hearing Alan's madcap suggestion, the Enterprise Board booked me to deliver my training module in two different locations the following week. D-Day arrived, and I breezed into the room and addressed my first seminar audience.

I had become a corporate trainer almost overnight, because I had the chutzpah to believe that I could do it. Before long, I was delivering seminars all over the country. I received invitations to address national and international conferences. I started visiting the USA to conduct public seminars and workshops as well as in-house training for leading multinationals. Chutzpah is the only logical explanation I can offer for this rapid turn of events.

> **We must have the chutzpah to dream the boldest dreams and have the wisdom to see that we can only make dreams a reality with hard and focused work.**
> Dr. Johnetta Cole

Best-Selling Dyslexic Author

The story so far...

Getting published when, by all logic, you shouldn't be able to write at all, is quite an achievement. That's what happened to dyslexic Julie Ortolon, who until the age of 20 could not read a magazine article, fill out a job application, or even open a bank account.

Because Julie's dyslexia had gone undiscovered right through her schooling, she felt awkward, stupid, and scholastically inept. Since college was not an option for an illiterate high school graduate, Julie used her talents to become an artist, an activity that did not involve any writing. She worked in animation, T-shirt design and advertising layout.

Yet despite her dyslexia, what Julie really wanted was to write stories. Ever since early childhood, she had been creating stories in her head. Her dyslexia prevented her from transposing these stories to paper, since the very idea of typing words that made her dizzy was unthinkable.

The chutzpah moment

One summer, Julie's cousin Marita handed her a copy of Kathleen Woodiwiss' romance classic, *The Flame & the Flower*. Determined to master the mammoth task of reading the book, Julie discovered a system of pointing at the word, listening to Marita pronounce it, looking at every letter carefully, and memorising it.

Captivated by the story, Julie slowly taught herself to read. The next breakthrough came when Julie's husband brought her a computer. Using the spell-checker, Julie was at last able to release the stories that were clamouring to get out of her head.

... and the consequences

Julie produced one novel, then a second, and then a third. She even managed to find a literary agent, but publishers were not interested in her historical romance manuscripts. However, these rejections only made Julie more stubborn and more determined.

Having overcome the biggest obstacle in her life, dyslexia, she wasn't going to let rejection notes slow her down.

Julie continued trying, no longer caring how many years it might take. She wrote a fourth novel, and then a fifth. This one was a witty contemporary romance about a woman with the courage to go after a dream and the strength to demand it on her own terms. At last, a publisher emerged, and Dell Books published *Drive Me Wild*. The book was selected as a featured alternate by Doubleday Book Club, and also reached *USA Today*'s bestseller list. *Romantic Times* magazine gave Julie's novel a glowing review, and within 10 days of hitting the bookshops, the book went into a second and a third printing.

After I had been delivering training seminars for a few months, my friend Grainne Harte said to me: "Your material has great potential as a book". So I sat down over the Christmas holidays and wrote the manuscript for **Fire in the Belly**. I had never written a book before, but I didn't waste too much energy thinking about that. After all, I had written thousands of promotional texts for my clients.

I assumed that I would take the self-publishing route. But when the manuscript was almost complete, my almost 80-year-old father adamantly insisted that I contact a *bona fide* publisher. Although I felt he was displaying totally misplaced optimism and well-meaning loyalty and belief in his son, I nevertheless started looking around for a publisher.

Feeling that I had nothing to lose, I decided to send an unsolicited email to Oak Tree Press, Ireland's leading specialist publisher in the field of enterprise. My email read: "I've written a book that tackles a neglected aspect of the entrepreneurial equation. Are you interested?".

Brian O'Kane, the owner of Oak Tree Press, had the courtesy to email back immediately, "I have just written and published a comprehensive and definitive book about starting your own business in Ireland, and I don't think I've neglected anything". He was referring to his best-selling *Starting a Business in Ireland.*

Non-plussed and chutzpah-fuelled, I ploughed on. I sent O'Kane a synopsis of **Fire in the Belly,** and elaborated on my contention that too little attention is paid to the crucial emotional transition from the security of paid employment to going out on your own. I attached the list of chapters, and a couple of sample chapters.

Within minutes, O'Kane's response arrived in my email inbox. "Whoops, missed that!"

Oak Tree Press went on to publish **Fire in the Belly: An Exploration of the Entrepreneurial Spirit**, followed a couple of years later by **"My Family Doesn't Understand Me!" Coping Strategies for Entrepreneurs.**

Since I was a first-time author, Oak Tree felt that a full-scale book launch event for **Fire in the Belly** in Dublin was over-ambitious. So I decided to launch the book locally in my hometown. I had never actually been to a book launch, but it didn't seem like rocket science.

Since I didn't have any spare funds to finance the launch, I resorted to chutzpah.

I used chutzpah to persuade the County Museum that the launch of a book by a local author was an event of public importance, and that they should therefore waive their usual room-hire fee. I used chutzpah to persuade a client who produced smoked salmon to provide the eats for the event. I used chutzpah to persuade another client to donate the wine.

I used chutzpah to persuade the Chamber of Commerce to make this an official Chamber event and to circulate an invitation to all members to attend. I used chutzpah to persuade the organisers of the local International Maytime Festival to feature the launch in their official list of events. I used chutzpah to persuade the drama festival MC to announce the launch from the stage. I used chutzpah to persuade my bank manager that the bank should also contribute to the cost of hosting the launch.

I used chutzpah to persuade an event management client to provide huge clowns to greet the guests. I used chutzpah to persuade the local electronic and print media to feature the launch.

The upshot of this multiple chutzpah, as was reported in the local press, was that well before the advertised time of the launch, a record crowd of about 200 squeezed into the museum. My friend Alan, who had first pushed me in the direction of motivational training, came over from Scotland to take the role of (hilarious) MC. Over 100 books were sold, and Brian O'Kane got up and said nice things about me. And as I mentioned earlier, Rodd Bond gave me the idea to write a book about chutzpah.

Why You Can Never Get Lost In London

The story so far ...

No visitor to London can possibly find their way around the city without the A-Z map book. The extraordinary woman who created the A-Z was Phyllis Pearsall. She came from a wealthy family, she was a lady of leisure, and she certainly did not need the money. It all started when Phyllis found herself totally lost in the streets of London on a rainy autumn night in 1935.

Determined never to repeat this experience, she went out the next morning to buy a map of London. She was disappointed to learn that the most recent map available was 20 years old, and was woefully inadequate to the task of helping her find her way.

The chutzpah moment

Using very primitive means - a notebook and shoeboxes full of index cards - Phyllis began to catalogue the streets of London. She rose every morning at 5am, and set out from her bedsitter in SW1, trudging down street after street for 18 hours a day. Word soon spread about this strange woman on a strange quest, and bemused onlookers began following her around.

When we look today at the A-Z's comprehensive index, carefully drawn maps, interlocking labyrinth of roads, parks, railway lines and bridges, it is hard to believe that one woman, working alone, had the chutzpah to attempt to do all this without the help of a computer.

... and the consequences

Phyllis eventually sketched no fewer than 23,000 streets in her notebooks. An accident with the T to R shoebox nearly led to the omission of Trafalgar Square in the first edition. She walked a total of over 3,000 miles. "I would go down one street, find three more, and have no idea where I was", she said. Her only staff was a draughtsman borrowed from her mapmaker father, but she did nearly all the work herself: she did the research, chose the weight of the paper, chose the size of type, selected the copy for the cover, compiled and proofread the index, and even chose the name London A-Z ("I couldn't think of anything else").

When the bookshops greeted Phyllis' masterpiece with almost universal apathy, Phyllis decided to form her own company, the Geographer's A-Z Map Company, in order to publish, print and distribute the book. Despite a lack of any forward orders, she gambled on a print run for the first edition of no less than 10,000 copies. Her first breakthrough came when WH Smith agreed to take a consignment of 250 books on a sale or return basis. Phyllis delivered the books in a wheelbarrow.

The A-Z became one of the all-time best-sellers in publishing history (a staggering 65 million copies sold and rising), and its creator became a multimillionaire.

Once I started working on this chutzpah manuscript, I decided that Sir Richard Branson's entrepreneurial history is so full of chutzpah that he would be an ideal person to write the introduction. I enlisted the help of a colleague who had dealt with Branson in the past to help me get my manuscript on his desk. Although Branson loved what he read, for a whole load of technical and legal reasons, he was not free to write the introduction. But chutzpah had helped me reach the man himself.

An online ezine called *Moxie* recently caused a media stir by announcing that it would charge writers a $10 fee for the privilege of submitting articles (with no guarantee that the article will be accepted.)

One shocked freelance writer expressed his view that it was the height of chutzpah for Moxie to effectively get writers to subsidise its publication.

"Let me get this right ... I have to pay so I can work for free?"

In many ways, my chutzpah route to publishing mirrors my chutzpah route to copywriting over two decades earlier. I had followed the conventional route that society had mapped out for me, including 20 years spent in continuous formal education to train me to become a useful member of the workforce. I had also spent seven years in gainful employment.

But I was not a happy camper. The employment world that I had assumed was my natural habitat started to feel oppressive. I realised that I had developed an allergy to institutional rules and regulations. I resented being told what to do. I reached the conclusion that any boss I worked for was invariably going to be ... well, let's just say that any boss bound to be a lot less smart than me.

The bottom line was that I was becoming unemployable. All my instincts told me that for the sake of my mental health, I had to opt out of the employment world and strike out on my own.

What my instincts failed to share with me was which field of activity the fates had in mind for me. My professional qualifications were not a useful pointer. I had an MA in industrial sociology, whatever that means. I had never considered myself entrepreneurial material, so I never gave any thought to pursuing my own line of business. So, when I came to the conclusion that I had to be my own boss, I had no idea which avenue to pursue.

Several weeks of heavy-duty thinking and brainstorming failed to generate either an "Aha!" moment or a "Wow!" idea. I was living in Israel at the time and, one day, I was contacted by an Israeli friend who knew that I was bilingual in English and Hebrew. He asked me for help in writing a brochure text in English for an electronic car alarm he had developed for the export market.

He gave me the basic information in Hebrew, and I sat down and wrote the brochure, ignoring the fact that I had never before written a marketing or promotional text. Before handing in my text to my "client", I also threw in some suggestions for the design and layout of the brochure. The next thing I knew, his graphic designer commissioned me to write the words for other brochures.

The penny dropped.

I realised that I was sitting on an unexplored, unexploited, untapped and undiscovered reservoir of creative talent - the ability to write advertising copy.

Wait a minute, did I say creative? This word immediately generated cognitive dissonance. Had I not been specifically told by my teachers not to pursue a creative career? Had they not shared with me their opinion that I should never consider a career in writing, because I lacked imagination?

It was only after consigning this advice to the dust-heap where it belonged, that I was able to believe that I could indeed write the words for advertising, marketing and promotion, even though I had never done it before. Based on the overwhelming empirical evidence of a single graphic designer who commissioned me to write some brochures, I decided to skip the conventional route of working as a copywriter in an ad agency. Fuelled by an intoxicating mix of naiveté and chutzpah, I opened my own freelance copywriting agency.

> **I think the reward for conformity is that**
> **everyone likes you except yourself.**
> Rita Mae Brown

I discovered that the act of starting a new business consists of simply having business cards printed and an "Open for business" sign fixed on your door.

I also discovered that that's not enough. You need clients, too. I realised that I faced a small problem: how to explain to my target audience (ad agencies and design studios) why I was unable to furnish them with a portfolio of previous work or with testimonials from previous clients.

I knew that I would have to resort to chutzpah.

"Just don't ask to see my portfolio, because I don't have one", I would pre-empt prospective clients.

"So how do we know what you can do?", they would ask.

"You'll have to take my word for it", I would say.

"Give us one good reason why we should", they would say.

"Just try me", I would answer. "If you don't like my work, don't pay me."

This unconventional approach persuaded a sufficient number of clients to take a chance on me. They did like my work, they did pay me, and I spent the next 25 years running a freelance copywriting agency. At the last count, I reckon I had written (and sold) about 10 million promotional words on behalf of my clients. Not bad for someone who was specifically discouraged by his teachers from writing.

That Takes Ovaries!

The story so far ...

At the best of times, it takes grit and determination to have a book published. But it takes real chutzpah to write a book, to write a play based on the theme of the book, and to launch a global organisation inspired by the book – all from the confines of your bed.

In 1990, writer, women's rights advocate, activist and self-proclaimed rabble-rouser Rivka Solomon was diagnosed with a debilitating form of Chronic Fatigue Syndrome (CFS). Too weak to function, she had to give up her career in international politics, and she spent most of the next decade bedridden or housebound.

Against all logic, Rivka refused to give in to her illness, and pushed herself to write. She was so sick that she could often not function for days, weeks or even months at a time.

On top of all her other problems, she then developed a second disability, Repetitive Strain Injury. She could not hold a telephone, and for a whole year she could not type.

The chutzpah moment

Rivka eventually landed a book contract with a major publisher and, for the next four years, tethered to her bed, she collected real-life first-person narratives from women and girls about gutsy, outrageous, courageous and the in-your-face deeds they had done.

Rivka chose a wide spectrum of stories, from light and frivolous acts to fighting for human rights.

When her illness threatened to torpedo her book contract, Rivka sought a novel solution. She found six young women volunteers who would visit her at home and type up the material as she dictated it. Although Rivka would often collapse with exhaustion and crawl back to bed, the volunteers eventually finished the manuscript and handed it in to meet the deadline.

... and the consequences

Rivka's collection of gutsy stories was published as *That Takes Ovaries! Bold Females & their Brazen Acts* in 2002. In 2004, a Chinese version of the book was published in China.

It takes chutzpah – and ovaries – to choose to ignore the debilitating effects of illness and to turn her adversity into triumph.

Yossi Abramowitz was also engaged in a search for a particular man. After working in media for several years, Abramowitz decided to branch out on his own. He spotted an opportunity to launch an ezine targeted at the family market, and put together a comprehensive business plan. He decided that instead of seeking finance from the banks, he would seek funds from a business angel.

And not just any angel investor. Abramowitz knew exactly who his business angel would be - the CEO of a major magazine publishing company. He convinced himself that, if only he could get this CEO to read the business plan, he would be able to persuade him to provide the necessary financial resources.

All Abramowitz's attempts to arrange a meeting with the CEO failed. He never got past the gatekeepers whose job it was to faithfully protect the CEO from unsolicited requests for funding. Abramowitz tried to snail-mail the material. No response. He tried emailing the material. Still no response. He had the proposal FedExed to the corporate headquarters of the company. Still no response.

Desperate situations call for desperate solutions. Abramowitz hired an actor, dressed him in a Barney the Dinosaur costume, and placed a bouquet of balloons in one hand and the precious business proposal in the other. Abramowitz deposited Barney outside the entrance to the building, and gently shoved him towards the door.

The security guard at the front desk took one look at Barney, shook him by the hand, and waved him in. Everywhere Barney went, his fans greeted him with laughter. He entered the elevator. When he reached the executive suite on the top floor, his way was blocked by a stern-looking receptionist whose job it was to ensure that nobody, but nobody, who didn't have an appointment could get past. The young lady took one look at Barney, and threw her arms around his neck. "Barney", she cried, "you're my hero. I've been a fan since I was a little girl!".

And thus it was that Barney was able to make his way unimpeded to the desk of the personal assistant to the CEO. He handed her the balloons, gave her the precious business plan, and left the building. Where phone calls, the mail, emails and couriers had failed to penetrate the barrier, Abramowitz's chutzpah had prevailed.

That was not the end of the story. When the CEO finally took a look at the business plan, he dismissed it out of hand. He regarded it as totally unworkable. And no amount of Barney chutzpah could persuade him that the ezine business idea had any merit.

Happily, this is not the end of our story. When you are as intrepid as Abramowitz, you don't give up so easily. He eventually found another business angel to provide the funding for what turned out to be a very successful business venture. I quote this story in many of my training seminars, both as an example of chutzpah, and to make the point that chutzpah is not only about winning – it's a mindset.

I'll Only Show You The Manuscript On My Terms

The story so far ...

Marianne Gunn O'Connor had a fashion business in Dublin. It was the early 1990s, the Celtic Tiger had not landed fully in Ireland. Marianne's business went into liquidation.

Shortly afterwards, she was approached by a friend who handed her the manuscript of a novel in a paper bag, and sheepishly asked Marianne to read it. Marianne took the manuscript home, read it, loved it, and decided to see what she could do to make sure that it got published.

She sought advice from a friend about whom she should talk to. The friend was Patrick McCabe, the best-selling author of *The Butcher Boy*. McCabe suggested that Marianne should contact Peter Straus at Picador. She did so, and he agreed to read the manuscript.

The chutzpah moment

No one should have been happier than Marianne. On her first attempt, a respected publisher had agreed to read a manuscript. But when Straus asked for the manuscript, Marianne refused to hand it over, unless Straus agreed to meet her so she could give it to him in person.

Somewhat taken aback, Straus agreed to meet her the day before he was due to fly to America. Again Marianne refused, insisting that the hand-over take place on the morning of Straus' flight. And thus it was that Marianne had an early morning breakfast with Straus in Dublin Airport, shortly before he was due to fly.

... and the consequences

As Marianne explained later, "I had to make sure he had the manuscript on the flight." She knew that the chances of Straus actually reading the manuscript were higher if he was stuck in an aircraft above the Atlantic. Her gamble paid off. As soon as Straus arrived in New York, he sent Marianne a fax: "Don't go anywhere else with this, I'm buying it".

This marked the beginning of Marianne's career as a literary agent. One of her first clients was her friend Patrick McCabe. Given her propensity to use chutzpah, it should come as no surprise that, in 2002, Marianne pulled off a literary coup – securing a million-dollar deal for Irish Prime Minister Bertie Ahern's 21-year-old daughter Cecilia for her first novel *PS I love You*.

**The golden opportunity you are seeking is in
yourself.**
Orison Swett Marden

Chip Tarver was planning to write a book about how to
contact anyone, any time for any reason. He called his
book *First Contact Secrets,* which was aimed at providing
the most important keys to achieving real business to
business success and sustaining long-term business
profitability.

Tarver came up with an unusual technique for gathering
the relevant material. He decided that in order to make
his material even more authentic, he would contact
people he didn't know yet, and to ask them to contribute
their ideas on how they like to be approached by people
(like him) who have proposals to make.

He contacted dozens of the greatest business to
business marketers in the world, and persuaded these in-
demand and hard-to-reach people to answer a series of
questions he put to them: "What's the best way to make
a successful initial business to business contact on the
first try? What's the worst way to make an initial
business to business contact, that blows someone's
chances?".

No less than 43 of the very top names in marketing
responded to Tarver's request. Among the people
appearing in his book are Jay Conrad Levinson, the father
of Guerrilla Marketing; Ted Nicholas, the "King of Print;"
David Garfinkel, author of *Killer Copy Tactics;* Jimmy D.

Brown, the undisputed King of Viral Marketing; and Dan Kennedy, regarded as the guru of direct marketing.

Giving Away 1,000,000 Copies Of A Book

The story so far ...

Businessman and marketing writer Seth Godin was founder and CEO of Yoyodyne, the industry's leading interactive direct marketing company, which Yahoo! acquired in 1998. Claiming that most marketers continue to throw huge sums of money at old-fashioned interruption marketing, Godin wrote *Permission Marketing,* which was an Amazon.com Top 100 bestseller for a year, a *Fortune* Best Business Book, and was four months on the *Business Week* bestseller list.

His other books include *Survival is Not Enough,* with a foreword by Charles Darwin; and *Free Prize Inside,* which describes how every single person in an organisation is in the marketing department.

The chutzpah moment

Godin proposed that good ideas should become viruses. He predicted that influential "sneezers", such as first adopters and trendsetters, would broadcast good ideas to the people they interact with, and the ideas would spread into popular consciousness. To prove his point, Godin decided to give his book away. He released *Unleashing the Ideavirus* as an e-text, and no fewer than 400,000 readers downloaded the book in the first 30 days of its release.

... and the consequences

Unleashing the Ideavirus became the most popular ebook ever written. As friends told friends about it, a total of over 1,000,000 people downloaded the digital version of this book about how ideas spread. The book was featured in *USA Today, The New York Times, The Industry Standard* and *Wired Online.* The hardcover version of the book reached #4 on the Amazon Japan bestseller list, and #5 in the USA.

Richard F X O'Connor is no stranger to the world of publishing. He is both a writer and a publisher, and is a much-in-demand speaker on communications, marketing and writing. Yet despite all his impressive credentials and accomplishments, it is still the story of how he broke into magazine publishing that makes him most proud.

During his long and illustrious career, O'Connor was executive editor of Renaissance Books/St. Martin's Press, president of the Publishers Advertising Club of New York, and marketing director with Waldenbooks, then the nation's largest book retailer. While he was with Waldenbooks, he became the first book retailer ever to advertise on television.

O'Connor is also a best-selling author. Titles include *How to Market You & Your Book: The Ultimate Insider's Guide to Get Your Book Published with Maximum Sales.* He has appeared on *Donahue, Good Morning America* and *Larry King.*

Anyone who knows anything about O'Connor knows that he has always been passionate about dry-fly trout fishing. It was this passion that helped him make his breakthrough into magazine writing.

It all started when O'Connor discovered the Nirvana of fishing: Tim Pond Wilderness Camps, in a remote area of northwestern Maine. Burning with a desire to share this out-of-the-way haunt with readers of *Field & Stream*, O'Connor decided to merge his private passion with his ability to string a few sentences together. He sent an unsolicited inquiry letter to *Field & Stream* magazine, something along the lines of "Hey, I love this place and I'm going to write an article about it whether or not you guys are interested."

No one was more surprised than O'Connor when he received a letter back from the Managing Editor of *Field & Stream*, assigning him a reference number, and commissioning him to submit whenever the article was ready.

O'Connor describes this as "the most treasured of my writing accomplishments ... an example of what a little chutzpah will do."

Getting Past The Gatekeepers

The story so far...

Dennis P Kimbro had written what he regarded as a ground-breaking book on how successful Black Americans had achieved their dreams, and how other Black Americans could apply the same principles in their own lives. Kimbro now needed an agent for *Think & Grow Rich: A Black Choice*. The key lay with Kimbro's role model, the legendary best-selling inspirational author, Harvey Mackay.

If I can only get a few precious minutes with Mackay, Kimbro said to himself, he could give me pointers on how to approach an agent. Spurred on by this thought, Kimbro placed call after call to Mackay. But for three months, he failed to secure the appointment he so wanted.

The chutzpah moment

The reason Kimbro had been so spectacularly unsuccessful in tracking down Mackay was that his Mackay's assistant had successfully protected her boss from Kimbro. All of Kimbro's bamboozling seemed to have no effect. Then he remembered that Mackay himself had written that when you encounter a gatekeeper receptionist, you should find a strategy for working with the gatekeepers rather than circumventing them.

So Kimbro cultivated the receptionist, and asked her what it would take to get to talk to her elusive master. She let slip that her boss would be taking five flights over the next five days. After promising that all he was asking was five precious minutes with Mackay, Kimbro persuaded the assistant to give him the flight numbers.

Sure enough, on one of the flights, the indefatigable Kimbro finally got his chance, and plonked himself down in a seat next to Mackay. He introduced himself to his captive audience of one, turned the timer on, and proceeded to deliver his spiel, promising to finish within the five-minute limit.

... and the consequences

Naturally, Mackay was won over, and their five-minute chat marked the start of a fruitful friendship between the two men.

With Mackay's help, Kimbro did indeed find both an agent and a publisher. He published *Think & Grow Rich: A Black Choice*, which distills the secrets of success contained in the lives of peak-performing men and women.

By now, you can probably guess my next question.

That's right. If you needed funds to start your publishing empire, couldn't you have talked up your acquaintance with a bank executive, like Wendy Pye did when she wrote to a Hong Kong bank?

If you wanted to write novels, couldn't you have overcome your dyslexia and, like Julie Ortolon, challenge the odds and keep trying until your manuscript was accepted by a publisher?

If you decided to do something as bizarre as what Phyllis Pearsal set out to do, cataloguing all the streets of

London by hand, couldn't you too have created the Geographer's A-Z?

If you were confined to your bed like Rivka Solomon, couldn't you have found the strength to collect stories about gutsy women?

If your efforts to reach a business angel came to nothing, couldn't you have followed Yossi Abramowitz's example and sent Barney the Dinosaur to do the job?

If you wanted a publisher to read a manuscript, couldn't you have followed Marianne Gunn O'Connor's example and refused to hand over the manuscript until you were sure that it would be read immediately?

If you wanted to write a book about how to make first contact, couldn't you have taken Chip Tarver's route and asked dozens of business marketing gurus what makes them respond to unsolicited communications?

If you wanted to prove that viral marketing really works, couldn't you have done what Seth Godin did, and given away hundreds of thousands of copies of his book via the Internet?

If you were a dedicated devotee of dry-fly trout fishing like Richard F X O'Connor, couldn't you have informed *Field & Stream* that you were going to write your article whether they accepted it or not?

If you were Dennis P Kimbro and you were desperate to have your manuscript endorsed by a well-known author, couldn't you have engineered a meeting with him?

As you have already gathered, I believe that you could have done all of these things. These chutzpah moments happened to people like you and me. When they put their mind to something, nothing could get in their way. Chutzpah played a major role in driving them, in pushing aside all doubts and doubters.

Chapter 6

Mile-high Chutzpah

It makes sense that chutzpah should figure strongly in the airline industry, which has a long history of attracting pioneering mavericks. From that first 12-second flight of the Wright Brothers, this is an industry where innovation is king.

Chutzpah is such a regular feature of the airline industry that there is even a website that awards regular Chutzpah Awards (although to be fair, the "winners" are usually deemed to have used chutzpah to hoodwink unsuspecting passengers!)

In *Air Transport World*, Leonard Hill wrote on Israel's national airline, El Al, headlined: "Chutzpah Airline."

Managerial grit that sometimes borders on cockiness seems to keep El Al Israel Airlines aloft against all commercial odds as perhaps the ultimate ethnic niche carrier. Maybe it's a mindset composed of equal portions of self-reliance and chutzpah (a Yiddish expression loosely translated as utter nerve or supreme self-confidence) that somehow translates into viability for the small airline with the outsized reputation.

Self-confessed maverick Herb Kelleher started out as an attorney. One day, as he was enjoying a drink with his pilot friend Rollin King, King turned over a cocktail napkin and sketched out a triangle. At the three corners of the triangle, he wrote Dallas, San Antonio and Houston. Kelleher took one look at Rollins' pictorial description of a lean and mean intrastate airline, and said, "Rollin, you're crazy. Let's do it." And they did it. The result: Dallas-based Southwest Airlines.

Southwest first launched in 1967, but it was not until Kelleher won a four-year legal battle that the airline took delivery of its first Boeing 737 in 1971. Since then, Southwest under Kelleher has been one of the most dynamic and responsive airlines in history.

Kelleher tells his people not to worry about profit, but to think about customer service. He claims that profit is a by-product of customer service, and not an end in and of itself. Chain-smoking, hard-drinking, hard-driving Kelleher has been described by *Fortune* magazine as "zany, with chutzpah".

Kelleher has made laughter, fun and chutzpah part of Southwest's culture. Prospective pilots have even been asked to don Southwest shorts, and only those who regarded the request as fun passed the interview. Kelleher once got involved in a legal dispute with another company over a trademarked slogan. He settled the case by publicly arm-wrestling the other company's CEO. Kelleher won.

One day, a Southwest vice-president complained that customers, gate agents, pilots and baggage handlers had more access to Kelleher than the vice-president did. Kelleher explained the facts of life to him very succinctly: "Let me explain this: they're more important than you are".

A 'C' Grade For A Multi-Billion Dollar Idea

The story so far ...

A few years ago, Tom Hanks starred in the movie *Castaway* about a FedEx courier who was portrayed as obsessed with time and with the pursuit of speed of delivery. This obsession came directly from the man who founded Federal Express, Frederick W. Smith.

While attending Yale, Smith had the idea of building a speedy and reliable national and international overnight passenger-less courier service based on air cargo.

This was a revolutionary concept, at a time when all cargo was still carried exclusively on scheduled passenger flights. Smith envisaged dedicated cargo planes that would fly at night, delivering and collecting parcels to and from a number of hubs. But when Smith wrote his ideas in his term paper, his Yale economics professor was singularly unimpressed: "The concept is interesting and well-formed, but in order to earn better than a 'C', the idea must be feasible".

The chutzpah moment

Despite the negative feedback, Smith refused to lose faith in his idea. He believed that, without a system like the one he was proposing, the economy would grind to a halt. He knew he had a winning idea, and was quite surprised that, by the time he returned from serving in Vietnam, no one else had yet proposed a similar idea.

When Smith announced that he was going to set up a cargo-only airline, the reaction was predictably negative. Everyone told him that his idea couldn't work, wouldn't work, and would end in tears. He leveraged $10 million of family money to raise a further $72 million in investment funds, and created Federal Express in 1973. His initial fleet of 14 jet aircraft flew between 25 East Coast cities.

... and the consequences

The FedEx route to global dominance was not always smooth. The freight-only airline was almost strangled at birth when the 1973 Middle East oil crisis made the company's operations uneconomical for the first two years. Smith endured a wave of "I told you so" accusations but, when the oil crisis eased, FedEx became the world's largest courier company.

After delivering only freight in the early years, FedEx added the overnight letter by 1981, and expanded overseas in 1984. At the last count, FedEx was a $20 billion business with a fleet of over 650 aircraft that move over 3 million packages every night in over 210 countries worldwide.

Michael O'Leary, the feisty boss of Ryanair, has openly acknowledged Southwest's Kelleher as his role model. O'Leary possesses chutzpah by the bucket full. It's written all over his face. In Yiddish, there is an expression for this - a "chutzpah poonem" – literally: chutzpah face.

When Kjell A Nordström and Jonas Ridderstråle used the term "outlier" to describe someone who dares to take risks, break rules and make new ones, they must have had Michael O'Leary in mind.

O'Leary has an irrepressible and irreverent sense of fun. Such is his success in promoting a populist image of underdog that ticket sales actually go up every time he is pilloried in the media. This is despite the fact that Ryanair has often been one of the most profitable airlines in the world. O'Leary probably pores over the morning papers, expressing expletives if Ryanair is not under attack.

The Sunday Times says: "For sheer chutzpah, Michael O'Leary has few equals".

In the immediate aftermath of 9/11, the aviation industry was facing meltdown. While other airlines tried to recover from the shock, O'Leary announced that Ryanair was giving away one million seats as a gesture of goodwill to anxious airline passengers. The *Irish Independent* wrote: "It is hard not to admire Ryanair boss Michael O'Leary's chutzpah in the face of possibly the greatest disaster ever to have hit the aviation industry". The blurb on the cover of a recent book about Ryanair speaks of the airline's "mind-boggling chutzpah".

Examples of O'Leary's chutzpah abound. Many people will remember Comical Ali, the name given to the Iraqi Minister of Information by the journalists covering the American war in Iraq? Comical Ali's whoppers used to add a farcical counterpoint to the more sober business of war reporting. When O'Leary felt that rival no-frills airline easyJet was publishing whoppers in their ads, he refuted their claims in full-page ads that sported a big photo of Comical Ali.

O'Leary also cheerfully breaks another cardinal rule in business: not to speak ill of your competition. He takes delight in poking fun at struggling airlines, and for years he publicly ridiculed Ireland's hapless Minister of Transport for what he saw as her inept handling of another of O'Leary's bugbears, Ireland's airport authority.

In 2002, during a head-to-head with German airline Lufthansa, the outspoken Ryanair chief offered to give away all its seats on 12 routes to Germany for one day if Ireland were beaten by Germany in a forthcoming World Cup match. O'Leary's only condition was that Lufthansa match the offer, by offering free seats for a day if Germany beat Ireland. The German airline did not accept the challenge, but once again O'Leary had obtained huge unpaid publicity for Ryanair.

More recently, O'Leary hit the headlines with a stunt that encapsulates his chutzpah. Dublin's roads are notorious for being almost permanently choked with traffic. The only vehicles that can move relatively freely and avoid the gridlock are the buses and taxis that travel in the dedicated bus lanes. As he made the daily commute from his native Mullingar, a provincial town, to his office at Dublin Airport, O'Leary used to look enviously at the taxis overtaking him on the inside lane.

So he bought a taxi plate (license), hired a cab driver, and became the taxi company's main (and only) passenger. This exploitation of a legal loophole left the National Taxi Drivers Federation and business executive rivals screaming about unfair tactics. O'Leary laughed it all off as sour grapes. Insisting that he was complying fully with the law, he managed to keep a straight face while claiming that he had simply bought the taxi as a good investment.

Not for the first time, the owner of O'Leary's Cabs of Mullingar had used chutzpah to attract huge free publicity for himself and his airline. The story dominated the Irish airwaves and print media for weeks, and it took a full two years before the loophole was plugged.

O'Leary's chutzpah efforts come fast and furious. In a 2003 publicity stunt, he presented the Irish government with a 1-metre long cheque for over $15 million to pay off his personal tax bill.

He Tried Harder

The story so far ...

Avis did not invent car rentals. That distinction belongs to Walter L. Jacobs in Chicago, who in 1918 started renting a dozen Model T Fords which he repaired and repainted himself. In 1923, he sold his car-rental concern to John Hertz, President of Yellow Cab and Yellow Truck & Coach Manufacturing Company. From that day onwards, Hertz has been the world's #1 car rental company. Yet it is Avis that really established the airport car rental business.

As a combat officer with the American Air Force during World War II, Warren Avis was frustrated by the lack of reliable ground transportation when he landed at various airports throughout Europe. After frequently finding himself stranded with no means of transport, Avis came up with a novel solution. He started stowing his motorcycle in the bomb bay of his aircraft, ensuring a quick getaway as soon as he landed.

When he returned home after the war, Avis looked around for a business venture to invest in. He remembered the problem he used to encounter at airports, and predicted that airports would be the brave new frontier for the auto-renting business, which at the time – with the exception of Hertz - did not enjoy a very high profile. It was such a hassle to rent a car that this was often something weary travellers did only as a last resort. The situation was made worse by the fact that car rental companies were typically located far from the airport at downtown used car dealerships, and frequently in the worst part of town. Many towns, especially those with mid-sized airports, had no car rental outlets at all.

The chutzpah moment

Avis' idea was greeted by a chorus of disapproval from bankers, lawyers, fellow businessmen, even best friends. Everyone predicted that he would bankrupt himself within a year.

Avis stuck to his guns. In 1947, using $10,000 of his own money, and a $75,000 note borrowed against his own name, he opened his first two outlets: at Willow Run Airport in Michigan, and Miami International Airport in Florida. He was so short on operating capital that he could only afford one employee at each rental counter per work shift. Hertz chose to stay on the sidelines as this cheeky young entrepreneur made a fool of himself trying to develop the airport car rental business.

... and the consequences

Avis proved everyone wrong. By the time he sold his company to pursue new entrepreneurial adventures, his car rental enterprise was a multi-billion corporation. Airport car rentals now flourish in 160 countries around the globe, employing hundreds of thousands of people, and generating hundreds of millions of dollar in new and used car sales.

Richard Branson is an entrepreneurial phenomenon. His life story, his business escapades, his daredevil stunts, and his lust for publicity have kept the media happy for over a quarter of a century. A book devoted to the success secrets of the business world's greatest brand builders, identifies "edgy chutzpah" as one of Branson's top 10 secrets.

Branson had the chutzpah to risk prosecution when he offered advice on venereal diseases through his Student Advisory Centre, which he established at the age of 17. He had the chutzpah to become the first mail order company in Britain to offer cut-price records. He had the chutzpah to approach politicians, rock music stars, intellectuals and movie celebrities to contribute articles to his magazine, *Student*, which he founded at the age of 16.

His chutzpah earned the now-famous comment from the headmaster of his school, Stowe: "Congratulations, Branson. I predict that you will either go to prison or become a millionaire".

Branson built an airline, Virgin Atlantic, which from the outset was successful in attracting passengers away from British Airways. He famously sued British Airways for resorting to dirty tricks to discredit him and his airline, and he won the case. To show his displeasure at the anti-competitive code-share proposals of British Airways and American Airlines, he had "No Way BA/AA" painted on the side of his aircraft.

He never missed an opportunity to get a swipe at British Airways. To celebrate the introduction of Virgin's first Airbus A340-600, which was at the time the world's longest airliner, he emblazoned on the fuselage the unforgettable slogan: "Mine's Bigger Than Yours".

Do you know of a good airport where I can sleep for free?

The story so far ...

In the movie, *Terminal*, Tom Hanks's character is based on the true-life story of an Iranian man who lived for four years in Charles de Gaulle Airport in Paris. All around the world, thousands of people sleep in airports before or between flights. The phenomenon is not new. But one young lady decided to turn this into a career.

Twenty-year-old Canadian student Donna McSherry went backpacking in Ireland in 1994. Like many other young travellers taking their first trip abroad, she was chronically short of funds. One night, she bedded down in Belfast's bus station, and discovered that she quite enjoyed it. The experience encouraged her to spend the night at Dublin Airport on her way home, rather than pay for a hotel in the city.

The chutzpah moment

A couple of years after her Irish trip, Donna was unemployed and had plenty of time to think. Musing over her airport insights, she decided to share her experiences with fellow-travellers.

She created her online *Budget Traveller's Guide to Sleeping in Airports*. The guide includes sleepability reviews of airports, bus stations, McDonald's, Burger King and hotel bathrooms.

... and the consequences

What started as something of a joke soon took on a life of its own.

To Donna's amazement and delight, hundreds and then thousands of fellow backpackers started e-mailing her with their experiences. The site expanded, offering useful survival tips, such as tying your luggage strap around your leg for safekeeping.

Donna then founded the Cheap Like Me Travel Society for "relatively sane people who do not want to spend a fortune when they travel. We embrace our travel cheapness with much honour, and are never ashamed to proudly declare 'Hey, I'm Cheap!'".

Donna's chutzpah-fuelled site has been featured in *USA Today*, the *Wall Street Journal*, *Time* magazine, and hundreds of other publications. Not surprisingly, Donna eventually did find a job – as a travel agent!

Stelios Haji-Ioannou, the son of a billionaire Greek shipping tycoon, entered the *Guinness Book of Records* when at the age of 28 he became the world's youngest international scheduled airline chairman, following the launch of easyJet in 1995. The airline's inaugural flights from London Luton to Edinburgh and Glasgow were in November 1995, and easyJet went international the following year with services to Amsterdam.

Within a few months of the launch of easyJet, the low cost carrier had become a thorn in the side of British Airways. The world's favourite airline did not take kindly to easyJet's brutally competitive fares. To combat the mass exodus of passengers on routes where easyJet competed with British Airways, BA decided to launch its own its own easyJet clone, the low-cost carrier Go in 1998.

Stelios reacted to this threat by applying to the High Court in London to prevent the new airline taking off. His objection was based on his contention that BA was only launching Go to undermine the competition.

When it became clear that his injunction against the fledgling airline had failed, Stelios made contingency plans. As soon as bookings opened for Go's inaugural flight, GOE103 from Stansted to Rome Ciampino on Friday May 22 1998, Stelios snapped up 10 £100 return tickets for the flight. He and nine colleagues turned up at Gate 14 in Stansted wearing distinctive bright orange boiler suits with words GO EASYJET emblazoned across them.

Once the Boeing 737-300 was airborne and the "Fasten Your Seat Belts" sign was off, Stelios and his friends started walking up and down the aisle, handing out flyers to the bemused passengers, many of whom were journalists covering the airline's launch. The flyer, which Go founder and CEO Barbara Cassani later described as displaying Stelios' "characteristic chutzpah", read:

> The unbelievable fare you are enjoying today is the result of a revolution led by easyJet which started in Europe some three years ago.

As the journalists piled into the back of the plane to interview the garrulous Greek, Cassani found herself alone at the front of the plane. Predictably, the headlines in the press next day focused on easyJet's hijacking of Go's inaugural flight.

The twist to this story is that in 2002, easyJet purchased Go to become Europe's biggest low fares airline.

Stelios loves controversy. When his easyCar company ran an ad in Holland: "The best reason to use easyCar.com can be found at hertz.nl", Hertz lodged a complaint. Stelios and a bunch of colleagues donned orange jumpsuits and demonstrated in front of a Hertz office in Amsterdam with signs reading, "What is Hertz afraid of?".

When Stelios stepped down from the chairmanship to pursue other entrepreneurial ventures, Richard Branson – no stranger to controversy - paid tribute to Stelios' chutzpah: "Millions of people who could not afford to travel before are now travelling - and he has done it with great style and panache".

From Hang-Gliding To Hampers

The story so far...

Twenty years ago, a young computer science graduate decided that she preferred the world of business to the world of IT. Actually, she preferred even more to hang-glide, a sport for which she developed a passion while at college. Liavan Mallin indulged her hang gliding passion by spending every weekend in the Wicklow Hills in Ireland. She also travelled to Wales, the Pyrenees and the Alps.

In California in 1989, she attempted the women's world distance record in Owens Valley. Her 106 miles beat the previous world record of 77 miles, and she later flew 132 miles, a record which stood for 10 more years.

One afternoon, sitting on a peak in the Wicklow Hills, waiting for the rain to clear, Liavan fell into conversation with two other glider pilots. They started fantasising about starting a seasonal business that would allow them to hang-glide all summer. Their brainstorming produced the idea of selling Christmas hampers.

The chutzpah moment

There and then, the three hang gliding enthusiasts decided to found Celtic Hampers. With zero experience and boundless enthusiasm, and with the help of a small loan from the bank, the three founders hit the doorsteps, delivering leaflets describing their hampers to 6,000 households, in Wexford and Dublin.

... and the consequences

In the first year, just 60 households placed an order for a Christmas hamper – a success rate of 1%. For just £2 a week, customers received enough turkey, ham, pudding, cakes and vegetables to get them through Christmas Day and the holiday season.

These first 60 customers were the key to building the business. Word-of-mouth spread the business, and new customers heard about the hampers from their friends and neighbours. Sixty customers became 600, then 6,000, and then tens of thousands. Thousands of women became Celtic agents. There were agent rallies, huge social occasions for the women to share experiences and feel part of a growing network.

The core business of the Christmas hamper company expanded to selling jewellery, toys and electronic goods. Corporate products followed and, by the early 1990s, Celtic Hampers had three catalogues.

By the time Liavan and her partners sold their company to Great Universal Stores, the US owner of Family Album, the company was handling 200,000 orders and 450,000 packages a year. Liavan went on to become a serial entrepreneur, founding companies in telecoms, property and IT in the US and Ireland.

You don't have to be an airline maverick to come up with outrageous chutzpah ideas. Couldn't you, like Herb Kelleher, have thought of starting a lean and mean intrastate airline?

Couldn't you, like Fred Smith, have foreseen that there was a future in the idea of a speedy overnight passengerless courier service based on air cargo?

Couldn't you follow Michael O'Leary's example and made a career out of being outrageous?

Couldn't you, like pilot Warren Avis, convert your wartime idea of using a novel means of transport to ferry you from airports, into a viable business proposition?

Couldn't you, like Richard Branson, make a career of self-promotion that turns you into one of the world's most recognised brands?

Couldn't you, like Donna McSherry, convert your hobby of bedding down in airports into a web guide for like-minded travellers?

Couldn't you, like Stelios Haji-Ioannou, constantly confound your competition by being prepared to push the envelope?

Couldn't you, like hang-gliding enthusiast Liavan Mallin, convert your passion into a multi-million hamper company?

In a word – yes!

Chapter 7

Wining & Dining Chutzpah

One of the best examples I ever saw of chutzpah in food advertising was a huge billboard in London that showed a breakfast cereal bowl packed with five huge Shredded Wheat biscuits. To the casual onlooker, this looked like an ad for Shredded Wheat. But when you read the tagline, you realised that this was not an ad for Shredded Wheat at all. It said: "I bet he drinks Carling Black Label".

For the uninitiated, this is a beer brand. The inference of the ad was that only a real man who drinks Carling Black Label could possibly eat so many Shredded Wheat biscuits at a single breakfast setting. Using Shredded Wheat to advertise beer – now that's chutzpah.

Another example of chutzpah advertising for a food product was the "I hate Marmite" campaign. Again for the uninitiated, Marmite is a yeast extract spread that people tend either to love or to hate – there is no middle ground. Advertised variously as "The Growing Up Spread" and "My Mate, Marmite", Marmite is very much an acquired taste. It is the food item most commonly missed and imported by British expatriates in other countries, and 16% of Britons take Marmite with them when they travel abroad.

For the 100th anniversary of Marmite in 2002, 33 London taxis were painted to feature the slogan, "100 years of HATE" on one side and "100 years of LOVE" on the other. It takes a whole lot of chutzpah to base an advertising campaign on the fact that half the population hates the taste of your product.

One Marmite TV commercial in 2004 plagiarised the Steve McQueen film *The Blob*, and showed people running in terror from a huge brown/black slime monster. When some of those running realise that it is actually Marmite, they jump headlong into the sticky mess with glee.

> **It takes chutzpah, a Yiddish word that means guts and moxie rolled into one, to establish a Jewish-style restaurant in Fairfax, where there's no Jewish population of note.**
> Review of a restaurant called Chutzpah

Moxie is also a food product that people either love or hate. This strange-tasting carbonated soft drink once ran advertising campaigns that warned consumers that they would have to "Learn to Drink Moxie". Moxie was originally very bitter and medicinal-tasting. One of its ingredients is the wintergreen herb, known as "moxie" when the formula was first concocted. This Algonquin

Indian word (literally "maski" or "medicine") could be the origin of the brand name Moxie.

Although you are unlikely to be familiar with Moxie unless you come from New England, many Americans recognise the word moxie (with a small "m") as a close synonym for chutzpah. The way this came about is interesting.

Dr. Augustin Thompson of Union, Maine, first marketed Moxie as a patent medicine in 1876 in Lowell, Massachusetts. It was sold as a cure for multiple ills, including "loss of manhood, paralysis and softening of the brain".

In 1884, Moxie was reformulated, repackaged and re-introduced as a carbonated non-alcoholic soft drink produced by the Moxie Nerve Food Company. Sales soared, and Moxie became America's first mass-marketed soft drink. Moxie remained the most popular soft drink until it was eclipsed by Coca Cola in the 1920's.

Moxie was heavily promoted in the early 20th century under the slogan: "What this country needs is plenty of Moxie!". Eventually, the word came to be an informal synonym for courage, guts and nerve.

If Moxie is associated with chutzpah-like moxie, the brand that took away Moxie's mantle as the leading soft drink, Coca Cola, has often displayed its own brand of moxie.

Addressing an audience of PR professionals shortly after the 2002 roll-out of Vanilla Coke, Bill Marks, Vice President of PR for Coca-Cola North America, emphasized the need for greater creativity in the PR field. He said that PR professionals should "try and find ways of putting chutzpah back into PR. Be a little pushy and get outside the proverbial envelope. But don't just think outside the envelope, act outside it too."

As the man credited with creating the early rumours and leaks that built such a buzz for the Vanilla Coke brand, Marks knew what he was talking about.

It all started when the *Financial Times* quoted a *Beverage Digest* report that Coke was planning to launch Vanilla Coke. With the impeccable credentials of the *FT* to back the rumour, the US media went into a frenzy as reporters scrambled to cover the story.

Faced with the challenge of maintaining the momentum until the actual launch of Vanilla Coke a full month ahead, Marks knew that he had to develop an event that would match the hype.

Marks' people found the solution while surfing the web. They discovered The Vanilla Bean Café in the Norman Rockwell-esque town of Pomfret, Connecticut, and Marks decided that this honest-to-goodness mom-and-pop café was a perfect off-the-wall setting that would drive maximum TV coverage.

The Vanilla Coke launch event hit no fewer than 1,500 local TV networks (95% of the TV markets) and 250 newspaper stories. Marks' PR efforts generated an unheard awareness level exceeding 40%. In Marks' own words: "First, there were the leaks. Then, our confirmation of the brand's existence. Third, the launch event. Our staff went and found The Vanilla Bean Cafe in Pomfret. That's outside the envelope. That's chutzpah."

When Kennedy Repealed the "No-Standing Law"

The story so far ...

The story begins in 1917, when for some archaic reason, it became illegal to consume hard liquor in Washington DC unless you were seated at a table. In other words, while you could imbibe as much as you liked during your meal, you were not allowed to have a drink standing up.

Early into his presidency, John F. Kennedy signed a bill that made it legal to serve Washington people standing at the bar with a drink.

Harvard Business School graduate Stuart C. Davidson was steadily working his way up the corporate ladder with Kidder-Peabody and Wettheim & Company. He watched this development from behind his desk at the bank. As a keen observer of the business scene, he assumed that the floodgates would now open, and that a horde of eager entrepreneurs would pounce on the opportunity offered by Kennedy's repeal of the standing-up law.

Convinced that that everyone else could see the same opportunity, he waited to see how many bars selling hard liquor would now sprout up all over the capital.

The chutzpah moment

Davidson waited. And waited. And waited. When he
finally concluded that no one else had grasped the
significance of Kennedy's bill, he pounced, and became
the first person in the field. The banker widely expected
to follow the conventional executive route abruptly left
his prestigious banking job and opened Clyde's
Restaurant & Bar.

... and the consequences

The first establishment in Washington DC where
customers could enjoy a drink at the bar before sitting
down for their meal since 1917, became an instant
success, and Davidson went on to open further
successful bars.

Stonyfield Farm is today the largest natural yogurt
company in the USA, and the #3 yogurt company in the
market. But it wasn't always such a large operation.

Samuel Kaymen was running the Rural Education Centre in
Wilton, New Jersey, when the funding dried up. In order
to keep going, Kaymen made yogurt. He wanted to gain
innovative and unorthodox marketing edge, so he brought
in serial entrepreneur and fellow environmentalist, Gary
Hirshberg.

In the early days, Kaymen and Hirshberg raised seven
cows in an 18-room Federal farmhouse. The yogurt
making operation was located in a barn. They made yogurt
according to their own special recipe, and would drive

into Boston where they stocked local supermarket shelves.

One day, when the company was in its infancy, Hirshberg was listening to a Boston radio talk-show. He heard the host make a startling boast: "I would rather eat camel dung than natural foods".

The next day, Hirschberg turned up at the radio station with two pails. In one was a gallon of his organic yogurt, and in the other was a gallon of frozen camel dung. Hirschberg challenged the startled radio host to put his money where his mouth was (or should that be, his mouth where his money was).

It is not known whether the hapless DJ actually consumed the camel dung, but the station was so taken with the story that they immediately broadcast details of Hirschberg's antics live. The story was picked up by hundreds of other radio stations, and soon everyone knew about the small Stonyfield Farm operation.

Hirshberg's chutzpah continued to accompany the company's growth. One day, he learned that buyers at the Bread & Circus supermarket chain were refusing to carry his product on the grounds that they didn't need another natural yogurt. So when friends asked Hirshberg what he wanted for his 30th birthday, he told everyone the same thing: "Go to Bread & Circus and ask for my yogurt". His chutzpah worked, and he got his products in the Bread & Circus door.

What do you do when you have started a new company and you have no money left for your marketing budget? Barry Potekin was a former stockbroker who lost his and his parents' money through investments that went wrong. He opened his first Gold Coast Dogs restaurant as an upscale fast-food operation in Chicago in 1985, and put on his chutzpah thinking cap in order to market and promote his new enterprise.

Every morning, Potekin left the premises of Gold Coast Dogs, hailed a cab at random in the street, and asked the driver to keep driving around the neighbourhood. By the time the cab arrived back at the restaurant, Potekin had pumped the driver full of information on all the reasons why he and the other cab drivers should eat at Gold Coast Dogs. In addition to paying for his fare, Potekin also handed the driver a five-dollar voucher for use at the restaurant.

The tactic worked like a dream. Before long, cabbies who wanted to use their vouchers were double-parking outside Gold Coast Dogs. And naturally enough, if any out-of-towners asked a driver for a recommendation on where to go for lunch, they soon found themselves being deposited outside Gold Coast Dogs. Potekin's unique brand of chutzpah self-promotion created the basis for what was to become a large chain of fast-food restaurants.

We Agree to Allow You to Become Our Sponsors

The story so far …

Anyone who watched the TV business reality show *Dragon's Den* will recognise millionaire Simon Woodroffe, who was one of the panel of business angels with pots of money to invest in candidates who could persuade the panel to give them their investment cash.

Back in the days when Woodroffe planned to open a new sushi restaurant in London, he needed to overcome the credibility gap with customers and building contractors alike. He knew that his marketing success depended on his ability to look as if he had prestigious multinational backers behind his Yo! Sushi restaurant. If he could get people to associate his restaurant with a major household brand name, his new enterprise would be taken more seriously.

Woodroffe approached Japanese auto and bike maker Honda. Not unnaturally, they refused to provide financial backing. However, he did persuade them to give him the loan of a motorcycle. He also managed to persuade All Nippon Airways to give him an upgrade when he flew to Japan to conduct his research.

The chutzpah moment

Turning his chutzpah full throttle, Woodroffe was determined to gain maximum leverage from Honda and All Nippon. He wrote to both companies, saying that as an expression of his gratitude for their kind gesture, he wished to appoint them as official sponsors of the restaurant – adding that they had a week to express any objection.

Whether the letters were ever read or taken seriously is
not known, but no objection was ever received.

... and the consequences

Woodroffe proceeded to milk the marketing value of
these two prestigious companies for all they were worth.
He displayed their names prominently at every
opportunity: on the menus, on the window, on the front
door, on the delivery bikes.

Suddenly, customers knew about Yo! Sushi. Suddenly,
investors and banks were taking note of the new sushi
restaurant with the famous backers. Woodroffe's
marketing chutzpah served him well, and he went on to
build a successful chain of Yo! Sushi restaurants.

Many food companies over-reach themselves in the
development stage, leaving very little budget for
marketing. BreathAsure (originally called BreathAssure,
but the company kept BreathAsure after the label
printer made a mistake) found itself in such a
predicament.

Founders Anthony and Lauren Raissen needed a fun and
inexpensive way of stimulating market awareness. They
knew that BreathAsure would be a winner, if only they
could get the word out. They racked their brains trying
to think of a way of making maximum splash with minimum
resources.

Then they came up with the inspired idea of taking a
stand at the annual San Francisco Garlic Festival in

Gilroy, the "Garlic Capital of the World". They handed out samples to people who had been tasting garlic all day, and a great buzz was created by this marketing ploy.

A talk show host who was visiting the garlic festival agreed to take the BreathAsure challenge – and he was so bowled over that he promptly featured the company on his show. All the local media picked up the story, and eventually the national media too. Soon, everyone had heard of BreathAsure.

"Well, I Know How To Bake Cookies"

The story so far ...

One day, at a party given in her home by Debbi Fields, a colleague of her economist husband Randy gently chided her for not doing anything with her life. This galvanised her into action. She decided that she would show everyone that she was not just an appendage to Randy's successful career.

Debbi's only problem was that she had no idea of what area she could get into. She had no career of her own. When she sat down to examine her options, she realised that the only thing that she was passionate about was baking chocolate chip cookies. She had developed an taste for entrepreneurship at the age of 13 when she sold her cookies at the Oakland A's baseball organization.

Friends tried to dissuade her, and even her adoring but world-wise husband rated her chances of success at close to zero. Debbi went ahead anyway, and managed to secure a business loan.

When Debbi opened her first Mrs Fields Chocolate Chippery store in Palo Alto, California in 1977, the sole product on sale was her home-made chocolate chip cookies. Husband Randy goaded her with a wager: "I'll bet you sales don't exceed $50 on opening day", he said. A sluggish start made it seem as if Randy was going to win his bet.

The chutzpah moment

Debbi was determined to attract customers by hook or by crook. So she filled a tray with cookies, and went round the streets of Palo Alto giving away free samples. People tried her cookies and were smitten. By the end of that first day, Debbi's sales had topped the $75 mark, and Randy had lost his bet.

... and the consequences

Debbi's company (now renamed Mrs Fields' Cookies) went on to become the premier chain of cookie and baked goods stores, with 1,000 outlets in 9 countries. With her business instincts and her great recipes, Debbi became a worldwide celebrity.

If starting a business is always a risky venture, starting a business 300 miles above the Arctic Circle, with no industry experience, little start-up money, and a hostile population, is extra risky.

When 50-something Fran Tate lost her engineering job designing airstrips and drilling sites for the US Navy, her employer offered her a desk job in Anchorage, Alaska. Fran wasn't interested, and chose instead to open a new business in Barrow, Alaska, a tiny and remote drilling town, perched on the edge of an eternally freezing ocean.

When Fran arrived in Barrow, the town had no running water or sewage services. To this day, the lack of roads connecting the town to the outside world means that supplies have to be shipped in by air. Ignoring advice from all her well-meaning friends and family, Fran decided first to tackle the water and sewage situation. Using trucks flown in from Anchorage, she opened a business supplying essential water and sewage hauling services.

Fran then decided that what the growing population of oil people and visitors in Barrow really needed was a Mexican restaurant. A friend of hers ran Old Pepe's Mexican Villa restaurant in Washington State, and he agreed to allow Fran to use his menu and his name. Pepe's North of the Border did not have an easy birth.

After 11 banks turned down her request for a business loan, Fran used her own savings to renovate an abandoned house. She ran out of cash before the work was complete, so she did something that not only took chutzpah, it also brought her to the attention of the law.

Desperate to make her new business profitable, she signed cheques to the tune of several thousands of dollars, even though she knew there was nothing in her account. Sure enough, one of her vendors complained to the police. Luckily, the Chief of Police knew Fran personally. Instead of arresting her, he gave her a week to make good on her cheques.

Pepe's North of the Border instantly became the hottest thing in town. Fran took in enough cash in her first week to cover her bad cheques. Fran got her payback when her business became so successful that it reached the pages of the *Wall Street Journal.* And she got her revenge by refusing to deal with local suppliers and banks that had refused to help her when she was building her restaurant.

The most famous fish and chips in the world

The story so far...

By all accounts, his own included, Harry Ramsden made the best fish and chips in Bradford, Yorkshire. For 16 years, this large exuberant man in his wing collar, starched apron and ribboned straw boater, worked hard in his small sit-down fish and chips restaurant.

One day, the family doctor announced that Harry's wife Beatrice had to move to the countryside to cure her tuberculosis. Harry thought his fish and chips career was over. As he said to himself, "Whoever heard of a fish and chip shop away from the busy metropolis?". Harry and Beatrice moved to White Cross, Guiseley, on the outskirts of Leeds. Harry borrowed £150, and in 1928 opened a small fish and chip restaurant.

Guiseley, the gateway to the Yorkshire Dales and the Lake District, turned out to be an inspired choice. Britain's day-trip industry was just taking off, and Harry's small but ideally located restaurant soon attracted a loyal following.

The chutzpah moment

But Harry had bigger fish to fry. He announced that he was building the biggest-ever fish and chip emporium in Britain, and he coined the phrase: "The most famous fish and chips in the world". Harry then had the chutzpah to persuade his suppliers that, because they had a vested interest in his success, they should participate in the funding of this project. His audacity proved successful, and his potato dealer, his fish supplier and his fat supplier loaned him the funds for the restaurant.

... and the consequences

When the magnificent new establishment opened in 1931, it really did become the most famous fish and chip restaurant in the world. Harry had a keen nose for publicity. He knew that he was helping his business by attracting so many famous film stars, politicians and business tycoons to the restaurant.

In 1952, in the twilight of his career, Harry dreamed up the mother of all chutzpah publicity stunts. By way of celebrating 21 years on the Guiseley site, Harry decided to sell fish and chips at the price (one and a half pence) they had been on 7 July, 1912, when he opened his first shop in Bradford.

In a single evening, Harry served more than 10,000 portions of fish and chips, and earned himself a place in the *Guinness Book of Records*. Brass bands, firework displays, traffic jams for miles around, and live coverage on the BBC were just part of a crazy day that still lives on in folk memory.

One of the best-known characters in the history of the restaurant business is Colonel Harlan Sanders, the man behind Kentucky Fried Chicken (or KFC, as it later became.) For the first 25 years of his working life, Sanders worked as a farmhand, streetcar conductor, soldier, railroad fireman, lawyer, insurance salesman, steamboat ferry operator and tyre salesman.

At the age of 40, Sanders opened a service station in Corbin, Kentucky, and began cooking for the travellers who stopped for gas. The service station had no dining facilities, so he served customers on his own dining table. When more and more people started coming just for the food, Sanders bought a motel and a 142-seater restaurant across the street. Over the years, he perfected his secret blend of 11 herbs and spices and the basic cooking technique to create his famous Kentucky Fried Chicken. In 1935, Kentucky's Governor Ruby Laffoon made him a Kentucky Colonel in recognition of his contributions to the state's cuisine.

Although the business thrived, post-war plans for a new interstate highway that would completely bypass the town of Corbin spelled the end of Sander's business. After paying his bills, the 64-year-old Sanders ended up flat broke. His dreams of retiring on the proceeds of his restaurant were in tatters, and he was reduced to living on his $105 Social Security cheques.

But it was not in Sanders' nature to sit around moping. Since the only thing he knew how to do really well was to cook chicken, he decided to try and sell his Kentucky

Fried Chicken recipe. Sanders kissed his wife goodbye, loaded up his battered old car with a pressure cooker, and set out to sell his recipe to the world.

He drove across the country, often sleeping in his car because he hadn't enough money for a hotel room. He would go into restaurants and cook batches of chicken. But although the restaurant owners and their employees loved the recipes, restaurant after restaurant balked at Sanders' chutzpah in demanding a nickel for every chicken sold.

In fact, Sanders suffered over 1,000 rejections before Pete Harman of Harman's Café in Salt Lake City agreed to pay for the privilege of using Sander's unique chicken recipe. Harman became the first Kentucky Fried Chicken franchisee, and soon restaurants were queuing up to buy a franchise.

Between the age of 64 and 75, Sanders had gone from being broke to becoming a millionaire. By the time he sold his interest in the business in 1964, Kentucky Fried Chicken had more than 600 franchised outlets in the US and Canada. By 2000, the KFC chain had grown to almost 11,000 locations worldwide.

Do something because it feels right, not because it makes sense.
Mary Hayes-Grieco

Targeting Pizza Customers as Potential Investors

The story so far ...

From an early age, Canadian Bill Mariani was able to come up with innovative ways of raising funds for his film-making activities. His film career began when he was 13. He wanted to make a short, but he could not afford the $50 to rent a video camera. In true Mark Twain style, Mariani persuaded 10 friends that they could star in a movie. All they had to do in exchange for this privilege was to pay him five bucks apiece. His friends came up with the funding, and Mariani had his first production.

Mariani never lost the film-making bug and, even while he was studying for his commerce degree, he continued to make videos. In order to fund his video-making and to pay for his tuition, Mariani started a lawn-mowing business. He would go door-to-door, just asking people if they needed their lawn mowed. Within a couple of years, Mariani had developed his lawn-care business into a larger business with two trucks and a partner. Needing extra funds, he branched out into pizza delivery.

The chutzpah moment

One day, it occurred to Mariani that his lawn-mowing and pizza customers were all potential investors in his movie-making company. He prepared an information pack, and after delivering a pizza and mowing a lawn, he would hand the customer the pack, and launch into a quick explanation of how he hoped to raise the finance for his movies by attracting lots of small investors. Then he would ask the pizza and lawn customer if he could call back later at a good moment.

... and the consequences

Impressed by Mariani's chutzpah, many customers were happy to take advantage of the tax write-off. Mariani estimates the pizza customers alone accounted for over $30,000 in investment. Fortunately for Mariani, the pizza company never received any complaints that one of their delivery boys was soliciting on the job.

He has made several movie shorts, and is considering getting into the film distribution field.

The rise to national prominence of caterer Russell Morgan was all due to a chutzpah letter. Morgan was born into a multi-generational entrepreneurial family. One grandfather had a sawmill that sold sawdust to pubs, another grandfather had an antiques business, and his parents ran their own hotel.

After completing his professional training as a chef in France, Morgan spent several years working in Hilton Hotels around the world before establishing his own full service catering company. Hungry to expand his fledgling business, he was constantly on the lookout for an opportunity to break into the big time.

One day, he chanced upon an article in the *Catering Times* about Brigadier Kit Barclay, the man responsible for commissioning catering companies for government functions. The brigadier was quoted as saying that government hospitality enjoyed the services of the three finest providers of food in London.

Russell sent a letter to him. "There has to be some mistake", he wrote. "You cannot be using the top three food companies, otherwise you would be employing my company."

Fully expecting that this cheeky letter would be ignored, Russell was astonished to receive an invitation from the brigadier to meet him in his plush Central London offices. After they had chatted amiably for a while about food, the brigadier dropped his bombshell: "I suppose we ought to give you a try, hadn't we?".

Against all odds, Russell had his foot in the door. His company received its first commission from the brigadier - to cater for an event in Lancaster House, the British Government-owned stately home near Buckingham Palace.

Other commissions soon followed and, before long, Russell's company was booked to cater for an event at Number 10 Downing Street, where Prime Minister Margaret Thatcher had just taken up residence after her victory in the general election. Russell's successful rapport with the Iron Lady led to a 10-year contract. Over the next decade, he catered to kings and presidents, prime ministers and international dignitaries. One unsolicited chutzpah-laden sales pitch - and what consequences!

It's time to make my usual observations.

If Bill Marks could think up the idea of using the mom-and-pop Vanilla Bean Café as the launchpad for Vanilla Coke, so could you.

If Stuart C Davidson could seize his chance when President Kennedy signed a bill making it legal to serve Washington people standing at the bar with a drink, so could you.

If Gary Hirshberg could promote his yoghurt by walking into a radio station with a pail of frozen camel dung, so could you.

If Barry Potekin could create traffic jams outside his Gold Coast Dogs restaurant, so could you.

If Simon Woodroffe could get Honda and All Nippon to become sponsors of his mew restaurant, without them being aware that they had agreed, so could you.

If the creators of breath freshener BreathAsure could attract national attention by taking a stand at the San Francisco Garlic Festival, so could you.

If Debbi Fields could turn her talent for baking chocolate chip cookies into the premier chain of cookie and baked goods stores, so could you.

If Fran Tate could open a restaurant in an Arctic location with no running water, so could you.

If Harry Ramsden could get away with calling his fish and chips "the most famous in the world", so could you.

If Colonel Harlan Sanders could have such belief in his Kentucky Fried Chicken that he approached 1,000 restaurants before finding one that would accept his terms, so could you.

If Bill Mariani could use his pizza delivery business to find potential investors in his film-making enterprise, so could you.

If Russell Morgan could write a cheeky letter that eventually led to his becoming Margaret Thatcher's favourite caterer, so could you.

They all used their chutzpah. So could you.

Chapter 8

Female Feistiness

Chutzpah does not recognise gender boundaries. Women are as likely to generate a chutzpah-fuelled idea as men.

One of the most famous female chutzpah stories involved a most unlikely cast of characters – the members of the Rylstone and District Women's Institute (WI)

When top movie actresses and models strip naked, we know that they are looking for a way to attract attention. But when the strippers are in their fifties, and are all highly respectable members of genteel British middle class society, there has to be something more to the story.

The picturesque county of Yorkshire in England lends itself to paintings and photographs of landscapes. So when the Rylstone WI members met to plan the group's next annual calendar in 1998, they were probably thinking of village greens, sheep and church steeples.

Hearing the president ask if anyone had photos to submit, Tricia Stewart leaned over and whispered a wicked suggestion to her friend Angela Baker. "Why don't we take a leaf out of the Pirelli calendar, and pose naked!" Later that evening, they shared this wild idea with Angela's husband John, Assistant National Park Officer for the Yorkshire Dales, who was then fighting a losing battle against leukaemia.

A few weeks later, John died at the age of 54. By way of consoling Angela, Tricia resuscitated her nude calendar idea. "As a tribute to John, why don't we pose in the nude, and use the proceeds from the sale of the calendar to raise £1,000 for the Leukaemia Research Fund?"

Her WI colleagues enthusiastically endorsed this crazy idea, and shooting began. So instead of the usual sunsets and landscapes, each monthly page in the WI calendar featured a naked WI lady carrying out a typical traditional WI craft such as jam-making, baking or knitting.

The ladies had hoped that their unusual exercise in chutzpah might attract a mention in a couple of local and national newspapers, and possibly even a TV appearance. But in their wildest dreams, they never imagined that their exploits would catch the imagination of a global audience.

The WI fund-raising exercise turned into an international phenomenon, and the nude calendar became a worldwide hit, with publicity in dozens of newspapers and magazines in Britain, Europe and America, as well as a movie that celebrates the fun escapade. To date, the WI members have raised close to £1 million for the fight against leukaemia. It is heartening to see how wild and zany ideas can lift a project out of the ordinary into the realm of the extraordinary.

"Please Help Me Settle My Debt"

The story so far ...

Few people have tackled the threat of bankruptcy with the chutzpah displayed by twenty-something Brooklynite Karyn Bosnak, who found herself completely broke in the summer of 2002. Karyn had landed a high-paying job during the economic boom, and proceeded to go on a spending spree. She ran up huge credit card debt, and everything came crashing down around her after she lost her job and ended up taking a job that paid about half. She was $20,000 in debt, and was desperate to find a solution.

The chutzpah moment

Lying in bed one night, Karyn came up with a plan. If 20,000 people gave her just $1 each, her debt would disappear. So she posted a message on a small low-budget website. After explaining how she landed herself in such a mess, Karyn wrote:

> "So I'm asking ... Please help me pay my debt. I am nice. I am cheery. I am the girl at the office that MAKES YOU SMILE. I didn't hurt anyone by spending too much money. I was actually HELPING OUT THE ECONOMY. Give me $1, give me $5 - Hell, give me $20 if you feel like it! I promise that everything you give me will go towards paying off my debt.

What's in it for you, you ask? I'll be honest ... nothing is really in it for you. But I do believe in Karma. If you help me, then someday someone might help you when you need it. SO HELP ME, and maybe someday, I'll be able to help you."

... and the consequences

If ever proof was needed that chutzpah pays, Karyn's story delivers that proof. The SaveKaryn.com site attracted 2 million visitors. People around the world were logging on and sending her money through PayPal and the mail, and the entire debt was paid off within weeks.

The story of Karyn's chutzpah received global media coverage, including the *New York Times*, *People*, and *Time*. She was interviewed on the *Today* show, and her site was named by the *New York Times* magazine as one of the "Greatest Ideas to come out of 2002".

Karyn so enjoyed her dialogue with all her well-wishers that she decided to create a new and improved website to serve as a resource for people who are financially strapped. The new site carries a banner message: "Thanks to you, I don't need saving anymore, but it's still the name of this website!" She is further exploiting her chutzpah by writing a book about the whole escapade.

One of the most unlikely pioneers of the automotive industry was a southern Alabama belle named Mary Anderson. Today, we cannot imagine cars without windshield wipers. But a century ago, even before Henry Ford had created his famed Model T vehicle, no one had solved the problem of removing rain and mud on a moving vehicle's windshield.

One summer on a visit to New York City, Mary noticed that streetcar drivers had to get out of their seats periodically and wipe the windshield in order to see out. This intrigued Mary. After all, she reasoned, if drivers have to wipe dust off the windows on normal days, they would have to get out of their seats even more often when it rained or snowed.

Although all the (male) experts predicted that any device that moved across the windshield was bound to distract drivers, Mary was not to be put off. Using all her chutzpah and determination, Mary went ahead and designed a device activated by a manual lever inside the car. The lever operated a spring-loaded swinging arm with a rubber blade that would swoosh over the windshield and then back to its original position.

The patent for Mary's device was issued in 1905, and within 10 years, ridicule turned to praise and even envy as Mary's invention became standard equipment on all cars. It took a maverick woman with chutzpah to beat the men in their own exclusive domain.

A Business Opportunity Literally Underfoot

The story so far ...

I came across this case study when a young lady (we'll call her Judy) shared her story with the other participants in one of my training seminars.

Judy inherited a very large house, and the first thing she wanted to do was have the carpets cleaned. But when she phoned advertisers in the local *Golden Pages* classified telephone directory, she was shocked by the high prices they were demanding. Judy was simply not prepared to pay so much, so she decided to do the job herself.

She went back to the *Golden Pages*, looked up the machine hire category, and found a local company. When Judy arrived at the showroom, she found that the smallest carpet cleaner available for hire was an industrial-size monster. Judy loved the monster cleaner. She had real fun doing all her carpets. When the job was done, she duly returned the machine to the showroom.

A few days later, a visitor remarked on her clean carpets. When she heard that Judy had cleaned them herself, she asked how much Judy would charge to clean her own carpets. Judy calculated how much it would cost to hire the machine, added something for her time and effort, and quoted a sum that her friend immediately accepted. Back Judy went to the showroom. She hired the cleaner, did the job and returned the machine.

When Judy took the machine back after yet another friend had asked to have her carpets cleaned, she realised that she could make much more if she owned it.

But when she asked the showroom staff about the cost of purchasing one, they told her that the machines were specially imported and only available for hire.

The chutzpah moment

Somehow, Judy didn't believe them. Suspecting that the showroom did not want her to know the size of their mark-up, she tracked down the importers directly. They were delighted to give her a quote, and her suspicions proved well-founded. She could actually buy the machine for less than the cost of 10 hirings. She bought it, and her carpet cleaning business quickly got off the ground.

... and the consequences

Judy discovered her business opportunity literally under her feet, and went with her instincts, even though this was light years away from her previous experience and training. When she first informed her husband of her entrepreneurial plans, he was downright hostile and dismissive. Judy went ahead and did it anyway. She had the last laugh. Her business was so successful that her husband eventually swallowed his pride, and gave up his salaried job to become her sales manager.

One of the recipients of the Oprah Chutzpah Award is Milena Zilo. When she was growing up in her native Albania, Milena had a single ambition in life – to become a finance major. After she and her family moved to Denver, Colorado, her college of choice was the University of Denver. With her 3.5 average, two internships, and enrolment in "every single club", Milena was sure that she would be accepted to the university's highly-regarded finance programme.

When Milena received a rejection letter from the university, she was so utterly devastated that, for a while, she hid the letter from her parents. But instead of sitting around moping about her misfortune, Milena decided to embark on the path of direct action.

She turned up at the office of the university's vice chancellor of enrolment, John Dolan, and loudly announced that she would not leave the premises until Dolan admitted her to the school. But Milena had not reckoned on the vice chancellor's equally determined secretary, who thwarted Milena at every turn.

So Milena decided on Plan B. She grabbed a promotional brochure that featured Dolan's photo, and she started walking the length and breadth of the campus, looking for him.

When she succeeded in tracking Dolan down, she buttonholed him, and informed him that a terrible mistake had been made. "All I want is 5 minutes of your time", she said. Dolan agreed, and brought her back to his office. After Dolan listened to Milena's story, he examined the notebook of recommendations and achievements that she had brought along with her. Dolan stepped out of his office for a few minutes, and when he returned, he acknowledged that a mistake had indeed been made.

Dolan was so impressed with Milena's chutzpah that he even offered her a scholarship. As Milena said later: "If there's one thing I've learned, it's don't stop at the first letter of rejection; if it's something you believe in, you have to go for it".

As a direct result of Milena's determined chutzpah, the university changed its application procedures. Candidates are now given a personal interview before a decision is made on their application.

What Do You Do When The Bank Turns You Down?

The story so far ...

I met Grainne Harte when I first set up business in Ireland, and we soon collaborated on a wide range of jobs together. I always admired her gutsy, fearless attitude to life and work, and her willingness to take on anything and everything. After becoming one of the youngest-ever managers of any London ad agency, she had returned to her native Ireland in the mid-1990s due to family circumstances.

Grainne went to work temporarily in Dublin, but her ultimate goal was to look around for an opportunity to start her own business venture. Her experience in London at the cutting edge of the advertising business led her to believe that online travel booking was the trend of the future. She set out to create Ireland's first dedicated tourist and travel website specialising in the Ireland market.

In order to prepare herself to run her own business, Grainne had been attending free Start Your Own Business classes a couple of evenings a week after work in Dublin. One of the guest speakers was Head of the Small Business Department of a major Irish bank, and Grainne discussed her feasibility study with him.

When the time came to raise funds for her Gateway to Ireland website, Grainne's first port of call was her local bank branch, which gave her a less than enthusiastic welcome. Not only did they turn down her request for start-up finance, they even refused to let her open a bank account!

The chutzpah moment

Now, it so happened that the offending bank was the same bank that employed the Head of the Small Business Department whose lectures Grainne had attended.

She called him. "Do you remember what you said we should do if a bank branch flatly turns us down?", asked Grainne.

"I do", replied her contact. "I suggested that you go over their heads and speak to head office."

Gathering all her chutzpah, Grainne said, "That's exactly what I'm doing right now", and proceeded to relate her experiences. He promised to look into the matter.

... and the consequences

The banking executive was true to his word, and the local branch bent over backwards to accommodate Grainne's needs. With her start-up finance now secured, Grainne set about actively convincing travel-trade advertisers to part with their money.

> Because she had flown frequently between London and Dublin, she called the local car rental company she used on every trip home. She was completely upfront with the CEO, and admitted that he was the first person she had approached to advertise on her website.
>
> He was so impressed with her honesty and her chutzpah that he decided to take a chance on her, and paid for his web-ad on the spot. Gateway to Ireland gained its first customer – and some very handy cash.

Austrian-born Marianne Pernold Young was a bored secretary in Washington. One evening, at a cocktail reception, she was asked by a stranger what she did.

On a total whim, Marianne boldly announced: "I'm a photographer". Imagine her reaction when the same guy called her a couple of days later, offering her an assignment to do an architectural shoot.

Rather than admit that she had merely been expressing a long-held daydream, Marianne took on the assignment. For that first job, she wisely decided to hire a professional to do the shoot. But she followed his every move, asked him countless questions, and closely observed his techniques.

Marianne's confidence grew, the daydream turned into reality, and before long Marianne was taking on regular freelance photographic assignments. The images of this totally self-taught photographer started appearing in prestigious publications, including *Newsweek, Business*

Digest, the *Boston Globe* and *Washingtonian* magazine. Her roster of clients included the American Society of Association Executives, and she went on to win several awards, including the 2001 Annual Spotlight on the Arts - Best Photography Exhibit.

The uninvited walk-in who became editor

The story so far ...

Getting a job with a company you really want to work for is a challenge. Getting a job with a company that has turned your application down is a bigger challenge. After studying in drama school and appearing briefly on the stage, Clare Booth Luce became a homemaker until her marriage ended. She set her heart on getting into the publishing business, and specifically set her sights on working for fashion magazine *Vogue*. She had high hopes of landing a job when she managed to secure interviews with both *Vogue* publisher Condé Nast and editor Edna Woolman Chase. But after the interviews, Clare was disappointed to learn that neither of them offered her a job.

The Chutzpah moment....

Clare obviously had a problem understanding the word "No", and she refused to accept that the lack of a job offer meant that she wasn't going to work at *Vogue*. So, one morning, she simply turned up at the *Vogue* office, and blithely informed an assistant that she had been hired. She found a vacant desk, and sat at it. By the time Nast and Chase realised that neither of them had hired her, Clare had made herself invaluable.

> ## ... and the consequences
>
> Clare was quickly promoted to editorial assistant, and within two years she was promoted to associate editor of *Vanity Fair*. Two years after that, she was managing editor. In just four years, Clare had leveraged her chutzpah to catapult her from uninvited walk-in to top person. She used this same determination to embrace several other careers. She became a playwright (*The Women, Kiss The Boys Goodbye*), congresswoman, journalist (*Mc Call's, Life*) and diplomat (US ambassador to Italy), and is regarded as one of the most influential women of the 20th century.

At 23, Shirley Halperin was three credits shy of graduating with a double major from Rutgers University. However, her real love was her work at a small record label in Manhattan, and her job as arts editor of the *Rutgers Review*. In order to give more time to her work, she decided to suspend her college enrolment temporarily. This proved to be strategically unwise, because the *Review* fired her on the grounds that she was no longer enrolled as a Rutgers student.

In Shirley's own words, "I got kicked off the staff of the school paper, where I was the best damn arts editor they ever laid their eyes on. In a fit of revenge, I decided to put out my own magazine". The magazine that Shirley decided to create was designed as an alternative-music information source for 16 to 30 year-olds.

Shirley had no business plan, very little money, zero experience running a company - but plenty of chutzpah.

Using just $1,700 in personal savings and $7,000 in donations from friends, family and music colleagues, she launched *Smug* magazine in 1995.

Shirley broke every rule in the entrepreneurial manual. Because she knew that young people never have enough money, she decided that her magazine should be free. She persuaded her 30 writers, photographers, editors, and designers to work for no reward other than by-lines, photo credits, college-internship credit, free film, and invitations to parties and concerts.

She openly informed readers that her intention was to educate them to appreciate bands they hadn't even heard of. Because these bands couldn't afford the heavy ad rates charged by the leading titles in the music field, Shirley's ad rates were a fraction of her competitors.

Shirley's bedroom became *Smug*'s nerve centre, and she even roped in her Goldman Sachs IT specialist father to keep the magazine's books. She got involved personally in every aspect of the magazine: setting story line-ups, writing and editing copy, selling ads, hiring staff, shooting some of the photos, overseeing pre-press and printing operations. She could even be seen delivering stacks of *Smug* around Manhattan.

Shirley's chutzpah paid off within just four issues. *Smug*'s circulation leaped to 20,000, readership reached 60,000, monthly ad revenues went from zero to $15,000, and the magazine won a prestigious local music award against its long-established competitors.

Sadly, despite her boundless enthusiasm and chutzpah, Shirley's innovative *Smug* music magazine could not survive in the publishing jungle of New York. After just 38 issues, *Smug* was history. I found the following message on the *Smug* website: "We are sorry to report that *Smug* magazine is no longer. After more than five years of hard work, devotion, and perseverance, we could no longer fund the publication as its growth very quickly out-paced our means".

Angie's List

The story so far ...

Anyone who has ever moved into a new area will be familiar with the feeling of not knowing whom to turn to for service. This was the problem facing Angie Hicks, an economics graduate of DePauw University in Indiana, when she moved to Bexley, Ohio.

As she grappled with the problems of settling into a new environment, Angie rapidly lost patience with the level of service she was experiencing from service providers.

She tried to be discerning, but it seemed that hiring someone to work around the home was mostly a matter of pot luck. There was no shortage of names to choose from in the Yellow Pages classified telephone directory, but Angie had no indication of the reliability of the service provider.

The chutzpah moment

Determined to something about it, Angie got together with a bunch of friends and neighbours and drew up a list of good and bad service companies.

Every time members of the group hired a roofer, a contractor or a Santa Claus impersonator, they shared their experiences with Angie. The feature that distinguished Angie's List was that it was a directory of service companies created exclusively by consumers, not by the service providers. The only way a service provider got on the list was when a consumer gave them a review.

... and the consequences

Very quickly, Angie's List became the most reliable source of independent, unbiased service ratings in Bexley. The idea caught on fast, and people in other communities started pestering Angie to open a chapter in their locality.

In each new city where Angie's List operates, the same ad appears in the local press: "Tired of Lousy Service? So was I, so I got together with my neighbours and compiled a list of our favourite service companies. We call it Angie's List. Now when we need a plumber, auto mechanic, painter or any other service company, we call to see who our neighbours recommend ...".

Angie's List, the company that started out with one woman's chutzpah, expanded into dozens of other markets around the US, and now has ratings on over 20,000 service companies.

Sara Blakely was no stranger to the world of self-employment. By day, she worked as a freelance sales trainer and motivational speaker. In the evenings, she was a stand-up comedienne.

For years, Sara had a bee in her bonnet - she had always yearned for pantyhose without feet. She had never actually seen anything like this, but this did not stop her badgering department stores and boutiques. The answer they gave her was always the same: "We don't stock anything like that, and to the best of our knowledge, nothing like it exists on the market. However", they would always add, "if we were ever to find a manufacturer who sold them, we would definitely stock them".

Sara discovered that lots of other frustrated women also wanted pantyhose without feet. She even met women who had resorted to improvisation by cutting off the feet of their hose and tying rubber bands around them.

Sara felt perfectly qualified to design and create the world's first footless pantyhose. But when she wanted to hire an attorney to patent her idea of footless pantyhose, the first few patent attorneys she approached showed her the door. And even the attorney who finally took her seriously was convinced at first that he had been set up by his colleagues or that he was the target of a *Candid Camera* stunt.

Sara knew that she wanted a name with chutzpah. Seeking inspiration from three of the world's most recognised brand names - Kodak, Coca-Cola and Xerox, she deduced that they all contained the "k" sound. She came up with the name "Spanks". This edgy, fun and catchy name eventually became "Spanx", and a new brand name was ready to take the market by storm.

Sara then came up with the slogan: "Don't worry, we've got your butt covered", and decided to tackle the packaging. Believing that buying a pair of pantyhose should be a fun activity, she ditched traditional design and adopted a bold new approach with a red package and three different illustrated women on the front.

Perfecting the prototype took over a year. Sara was obsessed with comfort and quality, and refused to give the OK until she herself was satisfied with the result. Finding a company to manufacture Spanx was another challenge. None of the manufacturers she approached took her seriously. She eventually found a manufacturer who believed in her innovative product and was prepared to take a chance on her. Spanx footless pantyhose started rolling off the production lines, to the relief of thousands of women the world over.

How Homesickness Led to a New Vacation Concept

The story so far ...

Some industries are born by design, others by accident. The low-cost escorted package holiday concept was definitely an example of how a new industry came about totally by accident.

Erna Low was Austria's national women's javelin champion when she moved to London to complete her doctorate in English literature. In 1932, the 22-year-old student became homesick for her parents back in Vienna, and decided to pay them a visit. The only problem was that Erna did not have a penny to her name. She was determined not to ask her parents for help, and she could think of no one to borrow the money from.

The chutzpah moment

Erna had a moment of inspiration when she came up with the idea of escorting travellers to Vienna. She would make all the arrangements, and use the commission she took from each traveller to pay for her own ticket. She placed a small ad in the *Morning Post*: "Viennese undergraduate taking party to Austria. Fortnight £15."

... and the consequences

Erna's eight-word classified ad received plenty of responses, and she accompanied her first group. Her no-frills escorted holiday to Austria offered excellent value for money, including travel, ski hire and instruction, 10 days' full board, and even some German lessons thrown in.

No sooner was Erna back in London after visiting her parents than she decided to do it again. And again. Before long, she gave up her literature studies, and started devoting herself full-time to this field. Her fledgling business was put on hold during WW2, during which Erna became a British citizen. After the war, Britain suffered from rationing and general privation. Once again, Erna came up with a novel idea – hosting house parties in big rented country houses.

Her next idea was no less innovative - Alpine skiing holidays, which she called chalet party holidays. Somehow, she managed to price these holidays at less than the Government's draconian £50 foreign exchange limit. By the time Erna sold her company in 1972, she had firmly established low-cost holiday packages as a major category in the tourism and travel industry.

These days, when you call a cheap flight call centre, the person behind friendly voice that answers you is as likely to be sitting in Bombay as in Birmingham. When you call American Express, the voice on the other end is as likely to be coming from Calcutta as Cardiff.

That's because the rise of outsourced call centres has created new job opportunities for hundreds of thousands of English-speaking Indians. For example, when I call the ebookers.com hotline, the voice on the other end doesn't just come from India, it also has a distinct Indian accent.

This gave Caroline Boudreaux, a former Fox TV sales executive, the idea of creating MiracleFoundation. This is a school that teaches Indians everyday English as spoken by modern day Texans, instead of the Queen's English taught in Indian schools by Indian teachers. Caroline has Girl Scouts taping stories in their Texan accent, as an aid to Indians who want to progress in this ever-expanding field.

Let's look at the chutzpah stories in this chapter.

The members of the Rylstone and District Women's Institute had the chutzpah to pose naked for a calendar that raised almost £1 million for the fight against leukaemia. You could have thought of that too.

Karyn Bosnak created a zany website that asked people to help her get out of debt. You could have thought of that too.

Mary Anderson first had the chutzpah to suggest fitting windshield wipers to motor vehicles. You could have thought of that too.

Seminar participant Judy had the chutzpah to turn her passion for cleaning her own carpets into a carpet cleaning business. You could have thought of that too.

Milena Zilo had the chutzpah to successfully challenge the university that had the cheek to reject her application. You could have thought of that too.

Grainne Harte had the chutzpah to contact a senior bank executive when she felt that she was being treated unfairly by her local bank branch. You could have thought of that too.

Marianne Pernold Young had the chutzpah to tell a stranger at a party that she was a photographer, even though she wasn't. You could have thought of that too.

Clare Booth Luce ignored the fact that *Vogue* turned down her job application, and had the chutzpah to turn up for work anyway. You could have thought of that too.

Shirley Halperin had the chutzpah to give up her studies at Rutgers to launch *Smug* magazine from her bedroom. You could have thought of that too.

Angie Hicks had the chutzpah to create a directory of service companies created exclusively by consumers rather than by the service providers. You could have thought of that too.

Sarah Blakely had the chutzpah to create her Spanx range of footless pantyhose, even though she knew nothing about the field. You could have thought of that too.

Erna Low had the chutzpah to turn her homesickness into an innovative vacation concept. You could have thought of that too.

Caroline Boudreaux had the chutzpah to create a school that taught natives of India to speak everyday English as spoken by modern day Texans. You could have thought of that too.

All these feisty women shared one important characteristic. They all ignored the safe option. They all chose unconventional solutions.

Chapter 9

Industrial-size Chutzpah

Chutzpah builds the muscles of enterprise.
Allison Kalloo

It is doubtful whether tyre magnate Harvey S Firestone was familiar with the term chutzpah, which in his day had barely infiltrated the American business jargon. But as he tried to build his company, he certainly displayed a healthy dose of chutzpah.

Benjamin Franklin is reputed to have coined the phrase, "Find out what the person you want to meet wants ... and give it to him". In the case of Firestone, this phrase should more accurately be paraphrased as "Find out where the person is going to be, and follow him there".

After considering the various options available to him for raising capital, Firestone decided that he preferred to sell stock rather than borrowing from financial institutions. He knew exactly whom he wanted to sell stock to: Will Christy, the most influential man in Ohio.

Firestone knew that, if he could persuade Christy to invest in his company, Christy would bring the financial clout and respectability needed to persuade others to invest. Firestone began to pursue Christy, who proved to be highly elusive. It was impossible to penetrate the army of secretaries that protected the big man.

Desperate to speak to Christy at all costs, Firestone resorted to old-fashioned espionage to discover his quarry's movements. By perusing the social pages of the newspapers, Firestone discovered that Christy and his wife were travelling from Ohio by train to California for a vacation. They were going to break their journey by stopping over in Chicago's Auditorium Hotel for a couple of days.

Firestone managed to reach Chicago ahead of Christy, and booked into the Auditorium Hotel before Christy. Later that evening, he checked to see whether Christy and his wife had in fact booked in that day. The last thing he wanted was to bump into Christy unawares, so he made sure to keep out of the way.

The next morning, Firestone got up early, and watched out of sight until Mr and Mrs Christy went to have breakfast. Quite by "accident", Firestone then met the couple as they went through the door of the dining room. He introduced himself, and they invited him to join them for breakfast.

By the time the meal was over, Christy had committed himself to investing in Firestone's company. This was to be the first of several major investments that Christy made in the company. Firestone's dogged determination to track down his quarry was fully vindicated.

Get Your Capital From Your Suppliers

The story so far ...

What do you do when you have zero capital to invest in your new company, and you have zero prospect of finding any? When Dennis Chang created his San Francisco-based company, Jasmine Technologies Inc., to manufacture disk drives and other Mac-compatible components, he faced this problem.

Chang's first challenge was how to finance the advertising. He had built his entire business plan around his ability to reach readers of *Macworld* magazine. He had to find a way of getting the ads on credit if he was to generate pre-paid orders. At first, *Macworld* laughed at him. But he persevered. He called the *Macworld* credit people on a daily basis. Finally, they agreed to give him advertising on credit. All they demanded in return was for Dennis to provide a personal guarantee of $30,000. The only way to meet this obligation was to be prepared to sell his house. He agreed.

Next, he needed a leasing company that would agree to rent him phones, copiers, computers and other office equipment. They too demanded a personal guarantee, so Chang recycled his personal guarantee to *Macworld*. The crunch came when the bills started coming in to Jasmine. Although Chang was able to pay the smaller bills, the company's rapid growth was now drying up the cash, and he found it hard to find money for the larger bills.

The chutzpah moment

Rejecting the classic strategy of trying to stretch - or even ignore - demands for payment, Chang took the opposite approach. He called his major suppliers every day. He returned their calls promptly. Whenever he managed to scrape together some money, he personally hand-delivered the cheque for part-payment to the supplier.

... and the consequences

Using the simple principle of getting all your capital from your suppliers, Chang succeeded in financing his fledgling company. And by his policy of constant communication with his suppliers and creditors, he kept them firmly on his side until the cash crisis eased.

Steve Latour was trying to persuade the 1-800-FLOWERS national flower company to handle his handmade Hawaiian leis. Time was running out. Latour knew that senior 1-800-FLOWERS executives were meeting to decide whether or not to carry his Hawaiian leis. He knew he had to come up with something outrageous to catch their attention. And he knew that he had to act quickly.

He went to an acting agency and hired an actor. He then hired a gorilla suit, as well as a white tuxedo and top hat. The smartly-dressed gorilla arrived at the Long Island head office of 1-800-FLOWERS, and handed out Hawaiian-style pizzas to all the executives who had gathered to make their decision.

Latour's chutzpah soon had everyone chuckling. The 1-800-FLOWERS executives loved his gesture, and they rewarded him with the contract he so coveted – to supply them with his handmade Hawaiian leis.

> **I firmly believe in chutzpah - that terrific Yiddish word for gall, guts, the drive to put yourself ahead.**
> Helen Gurley Brown

Something To Look At During An Elevator Ride

The story so far …

Who of us has not spent several seconds or even minutes inside an elevator, studiously avoiding the gaze of everyone else? We will stare mindlessly at the wall, we will fidget and we will check our shoe-shines - anything rather than look our fellow passengers in the eye.

As Michael DiFranza once again experienced the eye-avoidance phenomenon in an elevator, he thought that it would be a good idea if there was something worth looking at during the ride. By the time the elevator doors opened, DiFranza knew that he wanted to develop interactive screens in elevators using flat-screen technology and the Internet. The idea was to install these attention-grabbing screens on elevator walls, offering passengers weather, news, and traffic reports.

DiFranza formed Captivate Network, and together with his colleagues, he worked on the development of the concept for almost a year.

But the company's start-up funds were fast running out, and unless they could raise more money from venture capital firm Advent International, their future was in doubt.

The chutzpah moment

DiFranza sweet-talked the building manager of Advent's corporate offices in Boston into letting Captivate Network install a prototype screen in the elevator that serviced Advent's floor. On the very morning that Advent's investment committee was due to meet to consider Captivate Network's fate, the committee members were confronted with programming on the screen in their elevator. DiFranza and his colleagues had succeeded in bringing their message directly to the decision-makers. The interactive elevator screen rapidly became the talking point for the whole building.

... and the consequences

That afternoon, Advent announced that they and another venture capital company would provide a second seed round of $1.5 million. DiFranza's inspired chutzpah in commandeering the elevator in the Advent building won the day. The development work was swiftly completed, and Captivate Network went on to install elevator screens in Boston, New York City and Chicago.

When I was writing my first book, *Fire in the Belly*, I needed an example of chutzpah in order to illustrate the nerve and cheek you need in business. I came across the story of Cliff Hardcastle, and I have used this case study extensively ever since in my training seminars.

Hardcastle had worked for several years as an electrical engineer and a salesman. Frustration at his lack of access to the real decision-making circles in the companies he worked for prompted him to set up on his own. He established his Perdix import-export agency in his front room, and set about looking for clients.

He was delighted one day to receive a call from the defence division of Thorn EMI. The chief buyer there wanted Hardcastle to source some digital displays.

"Where did you buy these displays in the past?", asked an intrigued Hardcastle. "We used to get them from the Thorn subsidiary that manufactured them", replied the buyer, "but the plant has closed".

For some reason, Hardcastle had a hunch that the buyer might not be fully informed. He decided to do some homework on his own, and was delighted to discover that his hunch had proved correct. It's not that the buyer had got it completely wrong. The digital display subsidiary in fact had closed down in its previous location. However, the plant had relocated and was now operating in its new location on the other side of the country. Luckily for Hardcastle, news of these developments had not yet filtered down through the Thorn grapevine to the buyer.

Hardcastle knew an opportunity when he saw one. Speed was of the essence, so he rushed over to the relocated plant, showed them the specifications for the digital display he required, and obtained a price for the displays.

He then high-tailed it back to the Thorn buyer, and gave him a price proposal that included a hefty mark-up.

The buyer was delighted. The displays had exactly the specifications he needed (surprise, surprise!), and he could now supply the displays to the Thorn production department that had been bugging him for them. He happily handed over to Hardcastle the signed purchase order for a large quantity of displays. The opportunistic chutzpah that Hardcastle displayed helped him embark on a highly successful business career, and he went on to become a multiple entrepreneur.

It's the Early Bird that Catches the Worm

The story so far ...

It can be very frustrating trying to talk to someone on the phone, and failing to do so – not because they refuse to answer the phone, but because they are surrounded by people who filter the calls and prevent anyone getting through unless they are important enough.

Doug Mellinger was CEO of PRT Group, a software engineering services company in New York City. He wanted to appoint a Board of Advisors consisting of high-profile Chief Information Officers. He compiled a list of Chief Information Officers from *CIO* magazine, and tried to call the people on the list, in order to invite them to join his board.

His attempts proved spectacularly unsuccessful. It was not that any of them turned down his request. It was just that he never got through to them in the first place.

The chutzpah moment

One morning, Doug had a flash of inspiration. Maybe I could improve my chances, he thought to himself, if I catch the CIOs outside regular work hours.

The next morning, he started placing calls to the CIOs at 7.30am. His assumption was that diligent CIOs arrive at their office before the secretaries who intercept calls. Mellinger's assumption proved correct. One after another CIO personally answered the phone at this abnormally early hour of the day.

... and the consequences

Once Mellinger made a personal connection with the CIOs, they were very receptive to the idea. He was eventually able to convince several high-profile CIOs to join his Board of Advisors, and this high-powered group of senior executives continued to monitor PRT's progress as it grew into a global company.

Tony Stevens was a 13-year-old orphan who left school to join the Merchant Navy at the beginning of WW2. As soon as the war was over, he went looking for a job on dry land. The employment market was suffering from too many demobilised servicemen, and Stevens had to sell pints of his blood to finance his beer-drinking.

One day, Stevens walked into a small engineering firm in London, and literally begged the boss to give him a job. The boss turned Tony down on the grounds that he was not qualified, but he did not bargain for Stevens' dramatic abilities – or chutzpah.

Stevens burst into copious tears, and sobbingly pleaded to be given an opportunity to prove himself. The boss relented, and he was taken on. Twenty-five years later, he founded his own company, Planned Maintenance Engineering, with just one employee. He had no financing, but he did have a strong network of contacts. Stevens built his company into the largest private company of its kind in the UK, and by the time he sold it to Carillion in 2005, the business employed 2,000 staff.

There is something about inventors that captures the popular imagination. Ask anyone in Britain (and in many other countries too) to name a successful modern inventor, and the chances are that James Dyson's name will be mentioned.

After graduating from the Royal College of Art, Dyson became an inventor. Among his inventions were the innovative Ballbarrow, his widely-copied design for a wheelbarrow balanced on a sphere; the Waterolla water-filled plastic garden roller; and the Trolleyball boat launcher with ball wheels.

While renovating his country house in the Cotswolds in 1979, Dyson became exasperated with the poor performance of his Junior Hoover vacuum cleaner. He opened the machine, and discovered that half the suction was going to waste because of the bag.

There and then, Dyson decided to invent a bagless vacuum cleaner. His search turned into an obsession. He borrowed £25,000, he used £10,000 from his shares in

Ballbarrow, he sold his beloved vegetable garden, and he remortgaged his home. Over the next few years, Dyson and his family lived on just £10,000 a year as he worked obsessively to create a vacuum cleaner with no pore-clogging bags to impede suction.

No fewer than 5,127 prototypes later, Dyson finally got his Dual Cyclone vacuum cleaner to accelerate dirt and dust to speeds of up to 900 mph, creating powerful G-forces which spun out the dust and dirt into a clear cylinder that could be emptied, washed and replaced. When entrenched industry interests blocked his way forward in Europe, he took his invention to Japan, where his bagless vacuum cleaner started production in 1986, and won the International Design Fair prize in 1991

When UK production of the cyclonic cleaner began in 1993, sales went through the roof. The traditional vacuum cleaner manufacturers saw their sales plummet, and one by one they started introducing their own bagless models. Hoover later paid over $7 million in damages to Dyson when their triple vortex cleaner was found to be in patent infringement of the Dyson invention.

At any time during his long years of financial insecurity, Dyson could easily have given up his obsessive quest and continued to make a decent living inventing things. But the easy route was never an option, and his trademark blend of grit, genius and stubborn chutzpah kept him going.

The man who struggled financially for so many years single-handedly created the first breakthrough in vacuum cleaner technology since the first model was launched nearly 100 years earlier. Dyson is now one of the wealthiest men in Britain.

Dyson himself claims that he learned the importance of determination from long distance running, which he took up at school. According to fellow inventor Kenneth Grange, who invented the Kenwood Chef and the Kodak Instamatic camera, Dyson has "that wonderful cussed bloody-mindedness that won't back off in the face of a more orthodox view of things". This sums up very well the essence of chutzpah.

From Breaking Horses to Data Processing

The story so far ...

Most people have heard of Ross Perot, the maverick businessman whose fierce individuality and self-belief have repeatedly propelled him into the limelight. When two of his employees were taken hostage by the Iranian government in 1979, Perot directed a successful rescue mission, personally entering the Iranian prison where his associates were held. And, at an age when other people might be tempted to bask in the glory of previous exploits, he then became a presidential candidate.

An avid entrepreneur since the age of seven when he started selling Christmas cards, Perot went on to break horses, buy and sell bridles and saddles, and trade in calves.

His first job after leaving the army in 1957 as a career officer was to join IBM's data processing division as a salesman, where he remained for five years.

The chutzpah moment

But Perot grew increasingly disillusioned with the IBM bureaucracy. He believed he knew which direction the data processing industry was going, and he left IBM to start his own computer data service company. His schoolteacher wife Margot had infinite faith in him and loaned him $1,000 from her savings account. This allowed him to start his one-man data processing company in 1962, and he quickly progressed from offering consultancy services to offering mainframe computer access and programming services. He called his business Electronic Data Systems (EDS) - and a whole new business sector had been started.

... and the consequences

EDS became enormously successful, and within 20 years, Perot sold the company to his biggest customer, General Motors, for $2.5 billion. He joined the GM board, but then had the chutzpah to criticise GM management over the quality of GM automobiles. This falling-out led him to sell his remaining interests in EDS to GM for $700 million. The irrepressible Perot soon started a new computer service company, Perot Systems.

Irishman Maurice Muldoon worked in the sales department of the UK office of Canon, the global photocopier manufacturer. He was asked to set up the company's sales and telesales operation in Belfast,

Northern Ireland. Promotion beckoned once more when he was sent to his native Dublin to manage key national and government accounts for Canon Ireland.

But although Muldoon was happy to return to Dublin, he had already been entertaining plans to start his own business. He agreed to put his entrepreneurial plans on hold on condition that Canon accepted his condition - that he only intended to stay in the Dublin post for two years before branching out on his own.

In some companies, this kind of chutzpah could have pressed all the wrong buttons. But the Canon management evidently believed that two years with Muldoon was preferable to two years without him. Two years later, true to his resolve, he started preparing his exit strategy.

By now, he was totally familiar with the Canon product line, and he decided to leverage this expertise in his new venture. He made a novel two-pronged proposal to Canon Ireland: "Why don't we form a joint venture selling photocopiers and office equipment to the small and medium business market in Ireland's Northeast. Oh yes, I would also like to take three key staff off your hands to join me in the new venture".

Displaying remarkable foresight, Canon saw that Muldoon's chutzpah had business merit, and formed a joint venture with him. Sales rocketed. Muldoon had the temerity to ask. Canon had the foresight to respond.

The Pioneer of Guaranteed Next Day Business Mail

The story so far ...

Some niche markets are the result of deliberate planning. Others are discovered by accident. In Richard Trayford's case, it was very much the latter scenario.

Trayford had his heart set on a career in music, but he often had to resort to short-term stop-gap jobs in order to finance his fledgling music career. So when the opportunity arose to work for the Manhattan Borough Couriers bicycle-messenger company, Trayford planned to stay only a few weeks before starting his new job in music promotion.

After only a couple of weeks on the job, Trayford became increasingly puzzled by his employer's $1 overnight delivery rate. The company was offering this low rate anywhere in New York City as a teaser campaign to woo customers to its core same-day delivery service.

The chutzpah moment

Trayford realised that although there was plenty of competition among companies vying for the same-day business, very few companies were going after the next day service.

He believed that there was huge potential for a low-cost guaranteed next day delivery service, so he put his music career on hold, and borrowed $19,500 to launch Citipost. The company was built on the belief that business customers were looking for speed and reliability in delivering business mail.

The most obvious place to start his operation was Manhattan's Central Business District, so Trayford first targeted companies in publishing, media, and financial services whose needs revolved round the business district. He discovered that Random House needed hundreds of books delivered to reviewers and agents throughout Manhattan every single day. Trayford showed Random House that he could deliver their publicity material at half the price they were being charged by traditional courier services such as UPS and FedEx.

... and the consequences

Within four months, Citipost was handling all Random House promotional materials and, before long, the company's uniformed city walkers and courier drivers were making time-sensitive hand deliveries direct to addresses in key business districts. Citipost expanded rapidly, first around the USA and then internationally, and four days after the start of the new millennium, Citipost became a wholly-owned subsidiary of the British Consignia company.

Howard Jonas does not claim that he pioneered the telephone industry. He knows that that honour belongs elsewhere. But he did pioneer the callback system that paved the way to the cost of international telephone calls being slashed.

When he was still a student at the elite Bronx High School of Science, Jonas hired some of his teachers for his various enterprises. He dropped out of Harvard at about the same time as another famous student, Bill

Gates, in order to work on his own. He started an ad agency, a publishing firm, a New York City touring company, a brochure delivery business, and a mail order business selling bonsai trees.

His business dealings alerted him to the horrendous cost of international telephone charges. When he had been at college, Jonas had devised a system whereby he would call his parents collect, using a code name. They would refuse the call, and then call him back. This was an embryonic telephone callback system. Jonas believed that this system could be adapted for wider use.

One day, while driving through Israel's Judean Desert, Jonas was struck by the vision of a global phone company that would change telecommunications forever. Back in New York, he set about building on this vision. Things did not go well, and he soon became so dispirited that he was on the point of quitting. But since he had already booked a small exhibit space at Telecom '91, the once-every-four-years international telecommunications industry conference and exhibition in Geneva, he decided to give it one more try.

Jonas' Geneva experience did not start well when, following some incident, he was marched off the premises by Swiss gendarmes. Using his American publishing credentials, he managed to secure entry to the press room. He started distributing a press release to the business journalists from around the world who were tapping out their stories.

When Jonas tried to rejoin his colleague on their stand on the exhibit floor, gendarmes again tried to detain him. He ran back to the press room, yelling: "They're trying to get me. They're trying to shut me up. They want to squelch international telephone competition. No matter what they do to me, you've got to get the story out".

Just before he was again ejected by the gendarmes, he threw all his remaining press releases up in the air. This was a gift from heaven for the bored reporters, who descended on Jonas' stand. The story made the front page of the Telecom show's daily paper, and Jonas was readmitted to the exhibition. Thousands of visitors flocked to the stand.

Within days, the story of how this little company was cutting international telephone rates by more than 50% worldwide was featured in the international media. The *New York Times*, *Time* magazine, *Newsweek*, *Forbes*, *Business Week*, the *Economist*, the *London Times*, and the *Wall Street Journal* soon helped the company hit the big time.

Another person who left Harvard was Geoff Cook. When he was preparing his resumé as part of his application to Harvard, he realised that he would probably be including many of the same elements trumpeted by thousands of other applicants. They would all emphasise achievements such as student council president, captain of the tennis team, National Merit Scholar finalist, perfect 1600 SATs, and so on.

In order to stand out, Cook wrote in his personal statement about hiking up Mount Washington, comparing the hike to the pursuit of scientific study. The strategy worked, and he was accepted.

Once he was a student in Harvard, Cook noticed the desperation of applicants seeking admission to a top-ranked undergraduate or graduate schools as they sought help in writing their application essays. He spotted a business opportunity. Why not offer a service that would go beyond the kind of help that applicants got from parents, teachers and other mentors?

Driven by a mission to get America's youth into the college of their choice, Cook left Harvard in order to create CollegeGate.com. Within a year, his staff of 20 part-time editors had revised 1,500 application essays for applicants to colleges, business schools and graduate schools. Cook added credibility to his website by proudly reproducing Harvard's crimson and white colours. And although he regarded a Harvard degree as superfluous to his own personal needs, his home page informed potential clients that their essays would be checked by a "dedicated team of Harvard-educated essayists".

Harvard officials were not exactly delighted with Geoff's chutzpah, but the publicity surrounding their complaint about unauthorised use of their trademark only brought the site added publicity. Within a year, CollegeGate.com was editing more than 3,500 essays. Within four years, 200 freelance editors were processing thousands of personal statements every month.

Where Do You Go When You're 8ᵗʰ from Bottom in a Class of 1500?

The story so far...

Graduating eighth from the bottom of your high school class of 1,500 (or, put more kindly, in the top 99%) would not seem an obvious recipe for entrepreneurial success. Add severe dyslexia to the mix, and you can see why no one believed that Paul Orfalea would get very far in the business world. But they were wrong. Very wrong.

Orfalea always had an ambition to open up his own business. To compensate for his scholastic failings, he hired others to do his reading and writing. While looking around for a suitable business idea, he noticed that the college students in Isla Vista, the campus community of the University of California at Santa Barbara, were always looking for notebooks.

The chutzpah moment

Orfalea began selling notebooks on campus sidewalks. When sales started climbing, he rented a small garage behind a taco stand for $100 a month. He then spotted another opportunity – photocopying, and turned his tiny store into his first photocopy shop. He called it "Kinko's" after the nickname given to him by his college buddies because of his curly, reddish hair.

The original 100 square feet Kinko's had a single copy machine, an offset press, a film processing unit and a small selection of stationery and school supplies. As the store grew, so did the number of machines. At times, the space became so crowded that the copier was rolled out onto the sidewalk and used there for self-serve copies!

... and the consequences

Within three decades, Kinko's had expanded to over 1,100 branches in the US, UK, and several other markets worldwide. On his journey from hippie to high tech, Orfalea had started a new industry. Small business owners the world over know that they can pop into Kinko's 24 hours a day to prepare anything they require.

> **You need the fire, the talent and the chutzpah to succeed in business.**
> Kevin Reese

Many people know the legendary story of how the ubiquitous Post-It notes came into being.

Researchers at Minnesota Mining and Manufacturing (3M) had been working on a glue, but declared it to be a failure when it failed to dry like other adhesives. The reasoning was that no one would be interested in a glue that did not dry. But not everyone knows how the chutzpah of one 3M employee succeeded in getting management backing for this failed adhesive.

Art Fry was a member of a church choir. When he was looking for an easy way of marking places in a hymn book, he came across the failed experimental 3M adhesive that remained permanently sticky but was removable. He realised that these pieces of coloured paper had a wider use for writing reminder notes, and his challenge was to persuade the 3M top brass to adopt his idea.

Fry started by strategically distributing stacks of sticky little yellow reminder pads to secretaries around the company, based on his assumption that they were the best networkers. By regularly using the product as reminder notes for their bosses, the secretaries ensured that the reusable notes reached the attention of senior managers.

So far, so good. The notes were gaining in popularity, and Fry's plan seemed to be working. Just at the point when everyone was hooked on the reminder pads, he pulled a chutzpah rabbit out of his hat by stopping the supply of pads. He refused to renew the supply unless the top management officially gave the go-ahead to launch the product. Fry's chutzpah certainly had the desired result, and the "Post-It" note became one of 3M's biggest sellers. Since then, 3M has had a policy of constantly re-inventing itself, and a quarter of its annual revenue comes from products less than five years old.

Harvey S Firestone engineered a chance breakfast meeting with an influential businessman. His chutzpah succeeded, and the man invested in Firestone's company. You could have done the same.

Dennis Chang was determined to finance his business using supplier credit. His chutzpah succeeded. You could have done the same.

Steve Latour needed to attract the attention of the 1-800-FLOWERS, and sent a smartly-dressed gorilla to deliver Hawaiian-style pizzas to their executives. His chutzpah succeeded, and Steve became a supplier of Hawaiian leis. You could have done the same.

Michael DiFranza needed to convince a venture capital company to re-invest in his elevator interactive screen start-up. He installed a screen in the executive elevator. His chutzpah succeeded. You could have done the same.

Cliff Hardcastle needed to source some digital displays. His chutzpah in selling Thorn EMI displays back to Thorn EMI was the first in a series of successful deals. You could have done the same.

Doug Mellinger needed to contact high-profile Chief Information Officers, so he called them early in the morning when they answered their own phones. His chutzpah succeeded. You could have done the same.

Tony Stevens needed a job. When the boss of a small engineering firm turned him down, he burst out crying. His chutzpah succeeded in landing him the job. You could have done the same.

James Dyson was obsessed about developing a bagless vacuum cleaner. His chutzpah in sticking to his guns helped make him a multi-millionaire. You could have done the same.

Ross Perot sold his Electronic Data Systems to General Motors for $2.5 billion. His chutzpah in criticising them after he joined the board netted him a further $700 million. You might not be in the same league, but you could have found the same chutzpah to speak your mind.

Maurice Muldoon left Canon to start his own company. His chutzpah in his suggesting to Canon that they form a joint venture succeeded. You could have done the same.

Musician Richard Trayford had the chutzpah to predict that there was an underdeveloped market in a next day courier service. He later sold his company to Consignia. You could have done the same.

Howard Jonas wanted to promote his callback system at Telecom '91. His chutzpah in securing entry to the press room succeeded in gaining him international publicity. You could have done the same.

Geoff Cook left Harvard to edit application essays for college applicants. His chutzpah in claiming that the essays were checked by Harvard-educated essayists helped the company grow. You could have done the same.

Paul Orfalea was dyslexic and he graduated near the bottom of his class in high school. His chutzpah in ignoring these barriers helped make Kinko's a household name. You could have done the same.

Art Fry was convinced that there was a market for a failed 3M adhesive. His chutzpah in threatening to leave the company if they did not endorse Post-Its succeeded. You could have done the same.

None of these industrialists attended special chutzpah classes. None of them consciously decided to use their chutzpah. But at a critical moment, they used chutzpah to make decisions that would change their lives.

Chapter 10

Chutzpah for All Ages

**You're only given a little spark of madness.
You mustn't lose it.**
Robin Williams

Most people will have heard of Britain's King Edward VIII who abdicated in order to marry US divorcee Wallis Simpson. Edward's father, George V, was well-known in royal circles for his thrift and frugality. When the young prince once wrote from his boarding school that he wanted an increase in his allowance, the king sent a stern note of disapproval, urging the prince to change his ways and "learn to think like a businessman".

Edward took his father's advice to heart. Showing true entrepreneurial chutzpah, he sent back a note to his father in Buckingham Palace:

I have taken your advice. I have just sold your letter to a collector for £25.

Entrepreneurial chutzpah can manifest itself very early. When racehorse owner Victor Sassoon was a young eight-year-old, his parents allowed him to stay up late when they threw a large dinner party. There was one condition: he had to receive and hang up the guests' coats as they arrived. Unobserved, Victor slipped into the kitchen for a saucer. He then placed a single coin in the saucer, and left it on a ledge in the hallway.

When the first guest arrived, he gave the young Victor his coat, noticed the coin, and placed a larger denomination coin in the saucer. When the last guests had left the party, Victor's parents were astonished to find him counting his healthy profit for the evening.

Michael Dell started his entrepreneurial career when he was 10. His parents wanted him to be a doctor, but he had other ideas. By the age of 12, he had established his own mail-order business selling stamps, and was soon making thousands of dollars. While still in high school, he made $18,000 selling newspaper subscriptions. His selling urge did not desert him when he went to college.

Dell was supposed to be studying for his pre-med courses at the University of Texas at Austin in 1984. But all he wanted to do was fool around with computers. He had a nifty little business going in his dorm room #2713 in Dobie Hall. He upgraded PCs, and his sideline was soon pulling in $50,000 a month. So he quit college, moved to an off-campus condo, incorporated as Dell Computer, and pioneered the winning formula of selling PCs direct at attractive prices backed by good service.

That's chutzpah.

From Zero to One Million

The story so far ...

Ryan Allis was a normal 11-year-old, playing video games and living on a small island on the west coast of Florida.

Then he discovered entrepreneurship.

Allis' entrepreneurial career began when he provided computer help to people in his community. He soon progressed to website design, and was featured on the front page of his local newspaper.

He began working with a business owner who had not yet managed to record any sales for an innovative product in the nutriceuticals industry. During his senior year of high school, as Vice President of Marketing for the company, Allis created the company website, optimised it for the search engines, developed an affiliate program, and built joint ventures. Within one year, the company had over $1 million in sales.

The chutzpah moment

Not content with this success, Allis decided to become an entrepreneurial guru while still in his teens.

By the time he was 19, he was being hailed as the "most entrepreneurial teenager" in the United States and "the next Robert Kiyosaki".

In addition to his entrepreneurial pursuits, Ryan is also a syndicated columnist, an author, a columnist for *Brass* magazine, a publication covering all aspects of personal finance for young adults, and a speaker on the topics of entrepreneurship and web marketing.

He has written two books, *Obtaining a #1 Ranking in the Search Engines*, and *Zero to One Million*, a guide for aspiring entrepreneurs on how to build a company to one million dollars in sales. Ryan also publishes a monthly newsletter, *The Entrepreneurs' Chronicle*.

... and the consequences

At 19, Ryan was CEO of Broadwick Corporation, the developers of the IntelliContact Pro email list management software. He is President and CEO of Virante, Inc., a web marketing consulting firm for high potential companies, and the founder of the Entrepreneurs' Coalition, a non-profit organization dedicated to dedicated to teaching entrepreneurship in developing nations. He is President of the Carolina Entrepreneurship Club, and a research assistant at the University of North Carolina at Chapel Hill's Center for Entrepreneurship.

Newspaper tycoon David Sullivan was all of 12 years old when he decided that he was not satisfied with his meagre weekly pocket money. He faced a classic dilemma. He knew he had an aptitude for selling. He knew he wanted to start his own business. But, as any budding entrepreneur of any age learns very quickly, coming up with the necessary capital to fund a new enterprise is another thing altogether.

David decided on a novel solution.

"Whatever I sell will have to cost me nothing, because I cannot afford to pay for any stock", the 12-year-old business tycoon reasoned with himself. He set about finding something for nothing – and found it. Like many youngsters in his neighbourhood, David had been an avid football fan since he was very young. And like his friends, his hobby was collecting match programmes.

Keeping his eyes and ears alert at the matches he attended, David discovered that once a match was over, football clubs had no further use for unsold football programmes. He then proceeded to make the clubs an offer they could not refuse: "Let me have your out-of-date remainders for free - and I'll take responsibility for removing the programmes from your property".

The clubs were persuaded, and David's mail-order business commenced operations. He may not have known the word chutzpah, but he was applying it with gusto. He used his father's van to store huge quantities of programmes. This made his father a little nervous, because he was a serving member of the armed forces at the time, and it was strictly forbidden to use an army vehicle for commercial purposes.

Orders came pouring in for the starter-pack bundles of 50 programmes that David advertised *via* small ads in soccer magazines. He later expanded his activities by selling his programmes from stalls outside football grounds on match days.

David never looked back. He had started young, he was a natural salesman, and his chutzpah was to take him far.

The London Schoolboy Businessman with a Turnover of Several Million Pounds

The story so far ...

From a very early age, schoolboy entrepreneur Dominic McVey had developed a keen interest in stocks and shares. He read the *Financial Times* every day, and was so financially astute that his father allowed him to use his credit card to buy and sell shares on line. One day while surfing the web, McVey came across the website of Viza, the collapsible silver scooter manufacturer. He believed that scooters were going to be a huge craze in the UK, and he knew he could make money out of this.

The chutzpah moment

McVey decided to go into business. He was 13 at the time. He emailed the American manufacturer of the hugely popular Viza scooter to enquire about their overseas distribution plans. In no time at all, he had persuaded them to grant him the rights to become the only official organisation to distribute Viza scooters outside of America.

McVey developed an appropriate business structure for importing and distributing the scooters while vacationing with his family, but when he turned up for a meeting with the business advisor at his local bank, he was laughed out of the building. Undeterred, McVey raised money by running club nights, buying and selling tech stocks and importing a consignment of gadgets from Japan.

The second time he went to the bank, he had a proper business plan with him. The business advisor was certainly not laughing when he saw the projected figures.

McVey was too young to be a legal signatory, so his mother came aboard to co-sign the documents. He set up Scooters UK Ltd, and created his own website as the main sales mechanism. Working alone from his bedroom, he negotiated the distribution deals, handled the delivery of the imported scooters, coped with his many media appearances, and took care not to neglect his school studies.

... and the consequences

By the age of 15, the London schoolboy was running a business with a turnover of several million pounds. Someone with McVey's entrepreneurial gifts cannot sit still for long, and by the time he had reached the ripe old age of 17, he had already opened a web design business, was a regular magazine columnist, and had made inroads into the music business with plans for a weekly TV show.

When Mandy Fee's family asked her school if she could leave at 14 in order to help run the family-owned shop, there were no objections. Whatever potential they believed this energetic young lady had, it certainly didn't lie in an academic direction. Mandy worked in the shop by day, and in the evenings she worked in a bar.

It was here that she came into close contact with students at the local college. She discovered that they were having a hard time persuading TV rental companies to deal with them. Mandy went out and bought some second-hand TVs and VCRs, and rented them out herself to the students.

Next she discovered that some students were having problems finding digs. Mandy bought a trailer home, parked it in her back garden, and rented it out. Her knack for spotting entrepreneurial opportunities led her to start organising disco evenings in local hotels and nightclubs. Then she started managing bands and hiring out sound equipment. Then she started forming her own line dancing groups. Then she started hiring out DJs, bouncing castles and clowns.

Age was not a factor for Mandy. If young age is not a factor, nor is older age. Chutzpah can strike at any age.

We don't stop playing because we grow old.
We grow old because we stop playing!
Nana (age 103)

Ely Callaway was already in his sixties when he decided to try his hand at something new. He always had a knack of turning any entrepreneurial project he started into a roaring profitable success. After making his mark on the textiles and wine-making industries, he could have been forgiven if he was looking forward to the prospect of retirement and to playing endless rounds of golf.

The prospect of simply indulging his passion for the game by buying new golf clubs did not appeal to Callaway, so he decided to manufacture them instead. He founded Callaway Golf with just three employees. Over the next two decades, until he was well into his 80s, he turned his passion into a $6 billion business operation.

But having the chutzpah to embark on his third business empire when other people were happy to leave the hustle and bustle of the business world, was not enough for Callaway. Making money alone was no longer a challenge for hi. What he wanted was to make a revolution. He now devoted all his efforts to creating golf clubs designed to revolutionise the game.

In his own words, "If we don't make it better, someone else will".

The Callaway company introduced a series of clubs that transformed the market. First came Big Bertha, his tongue-in-cheek homage to the power of the WWI cannon produced by the Krupps ironworks in Germany and named after Baron Krupps' daughter Bertha. By allowing even mediocre players to get the ball airborne quicker and further, Big Bertha raised the game of hundreds of thousands of golf enthusiasts.

With his 80th birthday fast approaching, Callaway then introduced the ERC II driver - and landed himself in a storm of controversy. The all-powerful United States Golf Association wouldn't allow him to sell the ERC II to professionals because it did not conform to their testing limits. They then banned it from all tournaments.

With characteristic chutzpah, Callaway turned the tables on the USGA by persuading the Royal & Ancient Golf Club of St. Andrews, the governing body of golf outside North America, to recognise the ERC II as a legitimate club for all championship golf.

Starting a Business in Your 80s

The story so far...

Peter Drucker, the man who practically invented management science, died in 2005. For several decades, he travelled the world as a consultant to businesses and governments.

Peter was accompanied by his wife, Doris. Her job was to sit at the back of the auditorium, and shout "Louder!" or make hand signals to her husband to let him know that his voice was not projecting to the last row. Over the years, Doris wished that she could find a better way of providing Peter with feedback. At the age of 80-plus, she did something about it.

The chutzpah moment

The product that Doris Drucker had in mind was an electronic device with a microphone that transferred changes in the volume of the speaker's voice to a visual display in which lights of different colours would indicate different loudness levels.

In order to convert her brainchild into a marketable product, she turned for help to several consulting engineers. They did not take this elderly lady seriously, and refused to help. Doris then approached a retired engineer friend, and together they formed a company to develop the VISIVOX visual feedback monitor.

... and the consequences

Doris and her comrades produced prototypes, they acquired patents, and their product went on to sell in the hundreds.

Today, the VISIVOX is used also by speech pathologists who use the device to help people modulate their voice. If Doris Drucker had the chutzpah to start her first business when she was in her eighties, there is hope for us all.

These stories of youngsters and not so youngsters starting their own business serve as an inspiration to anyone of any age. The ability to make chutzpah-powered decisions is not limited by age. Age is just a red herring.

Chapter 11

Chutzpah –
A User's Manual

I have made chutzpah part of my *modus operandi*, part of my *persona*. I have chosen to integrate chutzpah into my suite of responses, into my thinking, into my mindset.

And I truly believe that everyone else can do the same.

So where do you begin?

We can see a clue in something that Steve Mariotti, who taught in some really tough New York public high schools, once told a business seminar:

> *Many kids branded as problematic by their teachers are in fact chutzpah kids who are gutsy, gregarious, resilient, audacious, affable, anarchistic and brazen – the same adjectives we use to describe our maverick entrepreneurs.*

Another clue is offered by Bonnie Shulman, professor of mathematics at Bates:

*I had a lot of chutzpah as a little kid. Maybe it's
natural in kids, but I didn't get it knocked out of me.*

This strikes at the very core of chutzpah. If we want to
find a way of accessing the chutzpah spark within us all,
the clue lies in kids.

It's natural for kids to want to do things that are daring
and cheeky. If we look back at the chutzpah stories in
previous chapters, so many of the chutzpah-inspired
adults behaved like wilful children.

I believe that when we behave with chutzpah, we are
reverting to the daring and cheeky children we once
were.

So what went wrong? Why do so many people lose their
chutzpah as they leave childhood?

The blame lies squarely with a society that actively
encourages kids to grow out of their childhood chutzpah.

A recent study showed that 96% of four-year-olds
believe that they can become anything they want when
they grow up, yet only 4% of 18-year-olds still believe
this to be true.

This is very sad. Because it means that as we become
adults, we learn how to conform to society's dos and
don'ts. For many people, saying goodbye to childhood
means saying goodbye to chutzpah.

So what do you have to do to repossess your chutzpah?

A good way of kick-starting the chutzpah mindset is to ask yourself:

"What would happen if....?"

"Wouldn't it be fun if....?"

"Wouldn't it be wild if....?"

"Wouldn't it be wacky if...?"

Just by asking these questions, you are already stretching your imagination, and you are opening the door for chutzpah to walk in.

Another way to kick-start your chutzpah is to say to yourself:

"If I had the balls, I would....."

"If I dared, I would..."

"If I had the nerve, I would...."

Again, just by saying this, you will already be imagining doing things you might not otherwise have dreamed of doing.

Imagination is the mechanism that triggers a chutzpah action. And since we all know how to access our imagination, we all have the potential to come up with chutzpah solutions, to experience chutzpah moments, and to be blessed with flashes of chutzpah.

First we imagine. Then we come up with the chutzpah response. The actual implementation is the easy bit.

Imagination is the beginning of creation. You imagine what you desire, you will what you imagine and at last you create what you will.
George Bernard Shaw

Life without chutzpah would be incredibly boring. So if you want to do things differently – try chutzpah.

If you want to make an unexpected and unconventional response to a situation – try chutzpah.

If you want to make an off-the-wall impact – try chutzpah.

We don't need permission from anyone to use chutzpah. The story is told of a child prodigy and Mozart:

Child prodigy: "Shall I write a symphony now, Mr. Mozart?"

Mozart: "No."

Child prodigy: "But didn't you write a symphony when you were my age?"

Mozart: "Yes, but I didn't ask anyone."

In the stories above, the chutzpah displayed by the protagonists usually elicited intense admiration.

However, you must also take into account that chutzpah has the power and the potential to prompt envy, resentment, jealousy, anger and belittlement.

This phenomenon is called *schadenfreude* – a German word meaning jealously of the achievements of others, and rejoicing in the misfortune of others.

> **Whenever a friend succeeds, a little**
> **something in me dies.**
> Gore Vidal

Many of us have experienced the guilty pleasure of schadenfreude, even if we're reluctant to admit it. The Australians call it the Tall Poppy Syndrome, the need to prove that someone who we put on a pedestal has feet of clay. The Irish call it begrudgery, sometimes described as Ireland's favourite blood sport. Under the rules of this sport, anyone who achieves a certain level of success deserves to be taken down a notch or two by those around him.

Begrudgery has a long history in the Emerald Isle, as we see from the remark of Samuel Johnson several hundred years ago:

> **The Irish are a very fair people, insofar as**
> **they never speak well of anyone.**

Bono (of U2 fame) illustrates the difference in attitude between the two sides of the Big Pond with the story of his first visit to Beverly Hills. He was being shown around by his American host, who prized individualism and romanticised the maverick figure of the mythic entrepreneur.

They looked at a beautiful new house up on a hill. There was a magnificent sports car outside, and by the side of a huge swimming pool stood the owner with a beautiful girl at his side.

"See that guy", said the American friend. "He built himself up from nothing, and now look what he's achieved". But Bono remembers thinking to himself: "Why has that bastard got all this and I don't?".

Sometimes, this envy gets the better of us. The *Today Show* host Bryant Gumbel was reprimanded after he sneeringly challenged Gloria Reuben for leaving her role as an HIV-positive nurse on ER to become singing backup for Tina Turner.

Writing about Canadian artist Toni Onley, Donald Todd said: "We admire (perhaps only secretly and with considerable envy) his flamboyant and highly successful chutzpah". Someone in an e-chat room wrote to Sarah Kerr: "I will envy you forever for coining the term 'chutzpah shock' ".

Fran Rooney knows all about begrudgery. To make his fledgling Baltimore Technologies' presence felt at the world's most prestigious security software event, the RSA Data Security Conference in San Francisco, Rooney took a huge stand, and threw a wild pre-conference party that became the talk of the show. Over the next few years, Baltimore punched way beyond its weight, and major US rivals were running scared of the Irish upstart company.

Then the bubble burst. In the wake of the telecoms crisis and 9/11, Rooney found himself ousted from the company that he had catapulted into the international arena. But the remarkable thing about this was how the Irish media turned on the business maverick when he fell from grace. There was zero acknowledgement that, after Baltimore was floated on the Nasdaq, its market capitalisation reached almost $10 billion. There was zero recognition that, in five short years, Rooney had taken Baltimore from absolute obscurity to becoming a global player.

So if you are thinking of adopting chutzpah as your mantra, avoid people tainted with negativity. Embrace the Buddhist concept of *mudita*, celebrating the success of others. Mudita means sympathetic joy, happiness at someone else's good fortune. The closest equivalent to mudita is the Yiddish word *nachess*, the special pride you feel for someone else's (usually a close family member) achievements and successes.

The good news is that the more chutzpah you display, the higher your tolerance for being ridiculed and laughed at.

**All great deeds and all great thoughts have a
ridiculous beginning. Great works are often
born on a street corner or in a restaurant's
revolving door.**
Albert Camus

As we saw in an earlier chapter, chutzpah is by no means
a new concept. Over the past few years, marketing gurus
and writers have used several other words to emphasise
the need to be different, the need to be unconventional,
the need to promote yourself in unexpected, fun and
quirky ways.

Conrad Jay Levinson created the term "Guerrilla
Marketing", which he defines as achieving orthodox goals
using unorthodox means.

Tom Peters created the term "the pursuit of wow", which
he defines as putting more passion into marketing.

Actor Paul Newman described his dressings business as
"madcap marketing".

Seth Godin created the term "Purple Cow", which he
defines as remarkable marketing. According to Godin,
brown cows are boring, purple cows are remarkable.

David Frey created the term "Controversy Marketing",
based on the controversy over his decision to promote a
manual called *The 12-Month Millionaire* on his website.
The author was Vincent Harper, who had had a run-in
with the Federal Trade Commission, took a plea bargain,

and spent a short while in jail. He discussed this openly in his manual. When some of Frey's subscribers objected to a convicted felon's book being promoted on the ezine, Frey published their comments, which sparked further controversy. Frey had originally estimated that about 20 people would probably buy Harper's manual at $200 a pop. In fact, he sold 213 manuals in four days.

Ryanair's Michael O'Leary talks about the advantages of being wacky in advertising.

Danny Brooke-Taylor and Tony McTear, creative directors of ad agency TBWA in London, talk of disruptive and naughty marketing. They claim that obeying convention does nothing for their clients.

Michaels and Karpowicz created the term "off-the-wall marketing".

If you think about it, they are all talking about different aspects of chutzpah.

All the inspiring stories in this book feature people who went the extra mile: people who employed, harnessed, leveraged, embraced, utilised, exploited, adopted and displayed their chutzpah.

Chutzpah means defying conventional wisdom and conventional logic.

Chutzpah means listening to your own inner voice.

Chutzpah means ignoring the negativity of friends and family.

Chutzpah means pushing against the grain.

Chutzpah means zigzagging around the doors that won't open.

Chutzpah means taking a leap of faith when the odds are against you.

Chutzpah means having the nerve to fulfil your dreams

Chutzpah means asserting that what you have to offer is valuable.

Chutzpah means having the guts to leave your comfort zone.

Chutzpah means walking boldly where others fear to tread.

Chutzpah means thinking outside of the box.

Chutzpah means allowing your imagination to run riot.

Chutzpah means a readiness to bend the rules.

Chutzpah means stubbornly charging ahead when reason indicates otherwise.

Chutzpah means a willingness to attempt things no one has ever tried before.

Chutzpah means shamelessly seeking out anyone and anything that helps us achieve our goal.

Chutzpah means seeing the extraordinary in the ordinary.

Chutzpah means overcoming the fear and doing it anyway.

Chutzpah means thinking innovatively and laterally.

Chutzpah means stretching the boundaries of creative imagination.

Chutzpah means making people sit and take notice.

Chutzpah means the extra ping, the special spark that helps us stand out from the crowd.

So nurture your chutzpah spark. Encourage it. Believe in your own chutzpah. Own it. Be proud of it. Believe that nothing is impossible.

Allow your chutzpah genie to escape from its jar. Allow your chutzpah to liberate your soul and help your imagination soar.

And above all: **May the chutzpah be with you!**

DO YOU HAVE A CHUTZPAH STORY?

Do you know any good Chutzpah stories
(either your own or someone else's)?

Do you have a new definition of Chutzpah?

Please email your material to
yanky@eircom.net,
and we will consider including them in
future collections of Chutzpah stories.

Other books by Yanky Fachler

FIRE IN THE BELLY – an exploration of the entrepreneurial spirit, is a no-holds-barred description of the emotional transition from employee to self-employed.
(Oak Tree Press, 2001)

MY FAMILY DOESN'T UNDERSTAND ME – coping strategies for entrepreneurs, challenges the myth that your family is always there for you when you decide to start your own business.
(Oak Tree Press, 2003)

THE VOW – rebuilding the Fachler tribe after the Holocaust, is the story of how Yanky's parents escaped to England from Nazi Europe before WW2.
(Trafford Publishing, 2004)

6 OFFICERS, 2 LIONS AND 750 MULES, tells the true story of Irish lion-killer Colonel John Henry Patterson, commander of the Zion Mule Corps, a volunteer transport unit that served in Gallipolli in WW1.
(PublishAmerica, 2006)

Yanky Fachler

Motivational
Training

with enthusiasm, humour & passion
www.yankyfachler.com

OAK TREE PRESS
is Ireland's leading business book publisher.

It develops and delivers
information, advice and resources
to entrepreneurs and managers –
and those who educate and support them.

Its print, software and web materials
are in use in Ireland, the UK, Finland,
Greece, Norway and Slovenia.

OAK TREE PRESS
19 Rutland Street
Cork, Ireland
T: + 353 21 4313855
F: + 353 21 4313496
E: info@oaktreepress.com
W: www.oaktreepress.com